The Business of Banking

The Business of Banking

Gerald Klein and Janice Lambert

Methuen & Co. Ltd

First published in 1987 by
Methuen & Co. Ltd
11 New Fetter Lane, London EC4P 4EE

© 1987 Gerald Klein and Janice Lambert

Typeset by Cambrian Typesetters, Frimley, Surrey
Printed in Great Britain by Biddles Ltd., Guildford and King's Lynn

All rights reserved. No part of this book may be reprinted or
reproduced or utilized in any form or by any electronic, mechanical
or other means, now known or hereafter invented, including
photocopying and recording, or in any information storage or
retrieval system, without permission in writing from the publishers.

British Library Cataloguing in Publication Data

Klein, Gerald
  The business of banking.
  1. Banks and banking—Great Britain
  I. Title   II. Lambert, Janice
  332.1'0941   HG2988
  ISBN 0–416–02132–8

Contents

Preface and acknowledgements vii

1 History of banking 1
2 Growth of the major banks 15
3 Money: the stock in trade of the banks 24
4 Who are the customers of banks? 36
5 The banker–customer relationship 52
6 Bank services to the customer 66
7 Banks and lending 89
8 Domestic services of banks 108
9 Foreign services of banks 126
10 Transfer of funds: the clearing system 136
11 Control of the banking system 162
12 Banks and competition 175

Appendices:
 I Relevant case law 205
 II Important statutes 214
 III Specimen examination paper 228

Index 235

Preface and acknowledgements

While the original reason for the writing of this book was to provide the candidates for the Chartered Institute of Bankers Stage I Banking Certificate with a book that would reinforce their studies for the subject 'Business of Banking', we felt after reading the manuscript the presentation was attractive enough to be a useful aid too for school or college students on courses such as BTEC, 'O' Levels, CSE, CPVE, etc.

We hope that students on courses that will eventually lead them into employment in the commercial or financial fields will find this book useful, not only to assist them in passing examinations, but as a foundation for continuing studies. For banking students, we believe that this book not only covers the syllabus as prescribed by the Chartered Institute of Bankers, but also provides the reader with a good background to banking law, which is essential for further studies for the banking diploma.

Our thanks must first be extended to Belinda Dearbergh and Sarah Cahill (Methuen & Co. Ltd) for their patience, guidance and occasional gentle pressure to ensure that we keep to the schedule.

We should like to express our thanks to the following for permission to quote copyright material: *The Banker* for Table 1; APACS Statistical Unit for Tables 2 and 3: the Bank of England for Figure 1: the Banking Education Service for Figures 5, 6 and 7 and the Chartered Institute of Bankers for the May 1987 'Business of Banking' examination paper in Appendix III.

To our friend and colleague, Len Stanley, National Westminster Bank, our grateful thanks for assistance in updating us on EFT-POS. Finally, our sincere thanks must go to Methuen's anonymous readers who so patiently went through the manuscript and gave us such helpful suggestions.

Janice Lambert
Gerald Klein

February 1987

1 History of Banking

In every town and city in this country you will notice that in the High Street or main shopping area there are banks. Many of them have names which you have seen over and over again, not only displayed on the walls of the premises, but also on television, in newspapers and other advertising media. Others may have names with which you are not familiar, yet they too serve the public as bankers.

Is banking a phenomenon of the present day? Certainly not. Banking in one form or another is as old as civilization itself. The earliest banks go back to biblical days, about 4,000 years ago. We also know from early records that the ancient civilizations of Rome, Greece, Babylon, China and Egypt all made use of banks.

How can the banks of antiquity be related to the modern computerized banks of today? It should be remembered that for all the sophistication of modern-day banking, the most basic service of all banks, no matter where or when they were in existence, is the safe-keeping of customers' funds. In early times most men and women were unable to read or write. Most did not need money – they worked for a master who provided them with food, clothing and shelter sufficient for their needs. The rich, the rulers, merchants and landowners had money in the form of gold and silver, so it was they who needed banks to look after their funds and valuables.

The literate men of the community were priests, and consequently they, with their ability to keep records, were the first bankers. Additionally, because they were priests they were considered honest and trustworthy. Not only could valuables confidently be left in their charge, but also temples, churches and other sites of worship were seen as places of safe-keeping. They were well guarded and it was a serious criminal offence to desecrate holy ground; for example, no one would dare break down the door of a church and destroy

2 The business of banking

any part of its interior – the punishment would probably be death.

As communities grew and prospered and began to trade with other communities, so the need for banking increased. On the other hand, as the early civilizations each fell into decline and were invaded by other tribes and countries, so their need for bankers decreased, alongside the falling prosperity of the community.

Very gradually, the business of banking was withdrawn from the hands of the priests and became part of normal trade and commerce. Indeed, one of the most successful periods for banks was in Italy during the eleventh and twelfth centuries, particularly in the states of Venice, Lombardy and Genoa; there banking prospered and grew to a considerable degree. Merchants in these states not only maintained the accounts of customers and looked after their funds, but were agents for collection, inasmuch as they originated the bill of exchange, which was used to facilitate the movement of funds and assist in the settlement of international trade within the Mediterranean area.

These days banks consider the latter function – to act as an agent for collection – to be a most vital service. Each working day, cashiers at every branch at every bank are taking in cheques in favour of their customers, crediting the account and sending these cheques to the clearing house for collection and final payment.

In Britain banking records could go back to the time of the Norman Conquest, when the chief bankers were Jews who both looked after their clients funds and were lenders of money. These loans were not for the purpose of trade as we would understand it today, but often requested by the nobles in order to equip their private armies or prepare for a crusade. The possibility of obtaining repayment of the loan was slight, so that the interest charged was, for those days, quite high. Because the interest rates were so high, the money-lenders were unpopular. Thus in 1290 Edward I expelled the Jews from England; they did not return until the seventeenth century. Between these dates, over a period of five centuries, villages and towns still had usurers who obtained large profits by their scandalous interest charges. While the government legally prohibited this trade, their efforts were without practical success. During the fifteenth and sixteenth centuries Britain saw the beginnings of industrial development, particularly in cloth-weaving, coal-mining and iron production. Large sums of money were thus required to finance these undertakings, and in response to this need the charging of interest on loans was controlled.

With the disappearance of the Jews from England in 1290, the Lombards and Causines established themselves as bankers. So great was their influence that a street in the centre of London – Lombard Street – was named after them. It was their custom to sit on a 'banca' or bench and transact their business. When the business failed, the bench was smashed and from this the word 'bankrupt' is derived. The Lombards carried out the business of money-changing and -lending to the merchants of London and anybody else who needed finance. Furthermore, they brought with them their skills in international trade, extending the methods of settlement between this country and the Continent by the use of bills of exchange (see Ch. 9).

It becomes clear that wealth was no longer only in the form of land held by country gentlemen and titled persons. Merchants and trades people held their wealth either in goods or cash. London was the trading centre of the country and the rich and powerful London merchants for a short time used the Tower of London as a refuge for their wealth. However, the monarchs of England – ever short of money – found it necessary from time to time to seize whatever funds were stored there. So the merchants, not wanting their wealth to be in constant threat of confiscation, looked for other places of safe-keeping.

Naturally enough it was the goldsmiths who provided the answer. They were accustomed to holding valuables on their premises. Like all basic bankers, their prime function was to look after the deposits of their customers and in exchange give them receipts for the money deposited. Very soon it was realized that instead of going to the goldsmith to withdraw funds, then handing it over to a creditor who would, in a short space of time, place the funds in the vaults of his own goldsmith, it was quicker and easier for a debtor to hand his

4 *The business of banking*

creditor the receipt for funds deposited. These receipts began to be passed from hand to hand, rather like money. To avoid continuous alteration to the document, the custom grew of drawing these receipts payable to 'bearer'. These, as you will realize, are the origins of banknotes.

The goldsmiths very quickly understood that, with the passing of receipts between debtor and creditor, it was unlikely that the whole of the funds deposited with them would be withdrawn at any one time, so that it was fairly safe for them to lend a proportion of the deposits to other people. These loans were repaid with interest, and goldsmiths soon began competing with each other to obtain deposits: thus, instead of charging customers for depositing funds with them, they tried to attract funds by offering interest on deposits.

As well as receipts being passed from person to person, rather like banknotes, a further development grew in the form of a letter drawn by the customer of a goldsmith, requesting the goldsmith to pay a certain sum of money to a named individual. This, then, was the forerunner of a cheque.

Eventually, some goldsmiths became small bankers, concentrating only on the business of banking. Sometimes they were very successful; at other times they failed, ruining their customers with them. Remember, these bankers in the fifteenth, sixteenth and seventeenth centuries, were merely sole traders or small partnerships. When there was a recession in a particular part of the country they, like the farmers or industrialists, suffered the same fate. There was no such principle as limited liability.

However, in 1694 an important event occurred: the establishment of the Bank of England. This was not a result of any desire on the part of the government to regularize the banking system. Rather, it was due to the fact that the sovereign needed funds to finance the wars of the Grand Alliance, and having cleaned up all other sources, decided to ask the merchants of the City of London to raise funds to pay the army. The merchants, being true to the Crown, raised by public subscription the sum of £1.2 million, but made this loan conditional. The conditions were as follows:

1 The funds were to be the capital for a new banking enterprise called the Bank of England.
2 The company was to be granted limited liability through Royal Charter.
3 Interest on the loan was to be 8 per cent per annum.
4 The Bank of England was to have the right to issue notes against the capital raised.

By these conditions the Bank of England was from the outset the foremost bank in England and has retained that position ever since. First, it should be noted that in those days £1.2 million was a vast sum of money, therefore it was financially stronger than any other bank in England. Second, unlike any other bank, its members had limited liability, so that they could not be made bankrupt should this new bank fail. Third, because it had the backing of the government, no other bank could really compete with it. Lastly, while all banks at that time were able to issue notes, but only against the gold and silver it had in its deposits, the Bank of England was able to issue notes to the amount of its capital, which in modern terms means that it was able to have a fiduciary issue.

The business of the Bank of England was divided. On the one hand, it acted as banker to the government, holding the funds of the various government departments and lending money to the government as and when required. On the other hand, it was involved in commercial banking practice, just as any other bank.

As confidence in the Bank of England grew, so it came to be the 'banker to the government' and began to circulate Exchequer bills. These were simply promissory notes issued by the government and were part of the national debt of the country, similar to Treasury bills today.

In 1718 the government put its borrowings on a more permanent basis. In response to a need for further finance, it issued government securities, which the Bank of England undertook to manage – that is selling the initial issue of stock and maintaining a register of stockholders, changing the names of the stockholders whenever stock changed hands. Further, the issue of interest warrants was part of the

6 The business of banking

responsibility of the Bank, and when eventually the stock had to be repaid this was done by the Bank of England as agent of the government. So it was that the Bank of England became the banker to the government and the manager of the national debt.

The Bank of England, like many other banks, had to overcome several crises. Whereas many banks failed when they could not meet their obligations, the Bank of England managed, sometimes by the skin of its teeth, to avoid disaster. A story has been told that when there was a rumour that the Bank of England could not meet its obligations, large numbers of its customers rushed to the counters of the bank to demand repayment of their funds. This the Bank of England was obliged to do in order to maintain confidence in its ability to act as a bank. However, the cashiers were instructed to pay out the various amounts demanded as slowly as possible, at the same time, in order to extend the queue, other members of the staff joined the queue, collected funds and promptly went round the back of the building, paid the money back in again, then rejoined the queue and continued the process for the day. When the Bank closed its doors at three o'clock, every person that had entered the bank had been paid. So it went on until the crisis had passed.

One of the worst periods of banking history was in the early nineteenth century, when many banks, particularly the country banks, had limited resources and, due to the law of those days, could not expand. Even as partnerships no more than six partners were allowed in a banking enterprise; in addition, there was no such thing as limited liability. This made banks vulnerable to the success or failure of industry and/or agriculture in their particular area. With all of them able to issue notes, some issued more than they were capable of supporting; there were, as a consequence, a large number of banking failures. In fact, in 1825 as many as seventy-three banks failed.

There was a succession of Acts of Parliament that tried to restore confidence in the banking system. One of the first measures was to allow the Bank of England to establish branches in various parts of the country. Another Act (1826) allowed joint-stock banks to be established – with note-

History of banking

issuing powers – providing they did not operate within a 65-mile radius of London. This was merely to allow the Bank of England to retain its supremacy in London and the home counties. However, shortly afterwards, in 1833, another Act did permit joint-stock banks to operate within the restricted area, providing that they did not issue banknotes. This, of course, foreshadowed the Bank of England's monopoly in note-issuing in England and Wales and the beginning of joint-stock banking.

Perhaps one of the major milestones in the history of banking, and indeed of the Bank of England, is the Bank Charter Act 1844. This Act was passed, as previous Acts were passed, to encourage confidence in the banking system. Again it must be emphasized that many smaller banks all over the country were going bankrupt. They were only sole traders or small groups of men who had just one office, or perhaps two or three, and were very vulnerable. The Bank Charter Act was a response to the uncontrolled issue of notes by such banks and the consequent tendency towards inflation and general lack of trust in the banking system. The basis of the Act was first to ensure that the Bank of England would eventually have a monopoly in note-issuing in England and Wales. It established that when banks went bankrupt or liquidated, their note issue was passed to the Bank of England. Similarly, when banks were merged, amalgamated or taken over by another, the right to issue notes was withdrawn. The monopoly took nearly eighty years to complete, when Lloyds Bank took over a West Country bank called Fox Fowler in 1921.

With the note issue safely under control, it was also decreed that the fiduciary issue of notes – that is the amount of notes in circulation without the backing of gold – should continue at the level of £14 million and should be backed by securities. To enable public and Parliament to keep a close watch on the amount of notes in circulation with and without the backing of gold, a weekly balance sheet was to be published for the two departments of the Bank of England. These departments are (1) the Issue Department and (2) the Banking Department. Since 1844 these balance sheets have always been published. Figure 1 shows a return made in June 1986.

BANK OF ENGLAND

Wednesday the 11th day of June 1986

ISSUE DEPARTMENT

	£		£
Notes Issued:		Government Debt	11 015 100
In Circulation	12297 432 465	Other Govt. Securities	5254 454 897
In Banking Department	12 567 535	Other Securities	7044 530 003
	12310 000 000		12310 000 000

BANKING DEPARTMENT

	£		£
Capital	14 553 000	Govt. Securities	467 785 932
Public Deposits— including Exchequer, National Loans Fund, National Debt Commissioners and Dividend Accounts	76 326 716	Advances and Other Accounts	931 522 344
Special Deposits		Premises, Equipment and Other Securities	942 066 845
Bankers' Deposits	924 760 691	Notes	12 567 535
Reserves and Other Accounts	1338 591 493	Coin	289 244
	2354 231 900		2354 231 900

Dated the 12th day of June 1986

D H F SOMERSET, Chief Cashier

Figure 1 *A Bank of England weekly return*

The Issue Department indicates on the liabilities side the amount of notes actually in circulation in this country and the world, and the amount held in the Banking Department. Notice that there is a contra entry on the asset side of the Banking Department balance sheet. On the asset side of the Issue Department balance sheet are the amounts of the government and other securities held by the Bank to cover the notes issued.

Looking at the Banking Department figures, the capital is the same as it ever was. The public deposits consists of the various government accounts. Special deposits were at one time taken from all banks in order to reduce the amount available for loans. With other controls now in existence, you will notice that this method of monetary control is no longer being used. Bankers deposits are self-explanatory. There are the deposits by all banks with the Bank of England, for clearing purposes, settlement of interbank indebtedness and other purposes. The reserves and other accounts merely represent the accumulation of profits. Listed on the asset side of the Banking Department are the holdings of government securities – stocks and Treasury bills – and a considerable balance of advances and other accounts, which are loans to discount houses and other customers of the Bank. Premises, equipment, and so on, are the fixed assets. Notes and coins are sums available for issue to banks and other customers.

One of the purposes of the Bank Charter Act was of course to control the money supply. The economists and banks of those days thought that if they could control the issue of notes and coins (money), they would be able to control inflation. How wrong they were. True, they controlled the issue of notes, but what they did not realize was that by creating deposit banking they were creating money. Bank deposits are also money. How does this work?

Let us take as a simple example the situation that there is one bank only and the total deposits are £100. From experience it is known that not all customers will wish to draw their money out at the same time. It is therefore possible for the banker to ensure that, if he has the confidence in his customers, he will always have sufficient funds available in his tills to satisfy their immediate needs. The remainder he can lend out to other customers, who for some reason or other need short-term loans. Consequently, when the banker decides that he need only keep £10 in his tills – to meet the needs of his customers – the balance of £90 will be lent. He will, in fact, create money.

What happens to the £90? Well, the customer who borrowed this amount will use it to purchase goods, say a new carpet. The retailer will then pay the cash or cheque into his account with the bank, therefore the bank has an additional £90 in the account of a customer. Using the same formula, only 10 per cent of this money need be kept in the form of cash; the balance – 90 per cent, or £81 – can be lent out to other customers, and so on, hence the bank or banks can create money. However, as you will see shortly, the Bank of England even today has control over the other banks and money markets.

Over a period of time the Bank of England very gradually withdrew from commercial banking and specialized in the function of being the central bank for the United Kingdom. Today the vast majority of its work is in this area. True, it has a few customers, usually large organizations, but it is not now possible for individuals to open an account with them, nor does the Bank wish to extend its commercial banking activities.

Since 1946, when the Bank of England Nationalization Act was passed, the Bank has been totally owned by the government. Its present-day functions are as follows:

1 *Banker to the government*: All the main government accounts are with the Bank of England. Funds are received from individuals and companies who have paid direct and indirect taxation. Through the Exchequer the funds are distributed to other government departments, who spend the money on such matters as education, defence, and so on.

The Bank will also arrange for the orderly borrowings of government. That is they will advertise the various stocks that government wish to issue, collect in these funds, maintain the stockholders' registers, issue the interest warrants at the appropriate time and at maturity arrange for the refund of the amounts due to the stockholders.

2 *Manages the Exchange Equalization Account*: With the commencement of the Second World War, the government had to impose regulations to stop the remittance of funds abroad – except for trade purposes or to help the war effort – and at the same time any funds that were coming into the country had to be surrendered to the government. These regulations were later to become the Exchange Control Act 1947. Any funds

History of banking

held by residents of this country, and any funds received by residents of this country, had to be paid into the banks, which then transferred the money to the Bank of England. The account used for this purpose is known as the Exchange Equalization Account.

Although we no longer have exchange-control regulations, the account is still used for the official reserves of currency and gold. It is through this account that the Bank of England will enter the foreign-exchange market to buy or sell sterling in order to prevent major fluctuations of sterling against other international currencies.

3 *Note-issuing authority*: As a result of the Bank Charter Act, the Bank of England is the only authority allowed to issue notes in England and Wales. Scotland, the Isle of Man and the Channel Islands still have their own note issue, but the amount issued is strictly controlled by the Bank of England.

The Bank of England owns its own printing machines and will print and circulate notes as needed. The main method of distribution of these notes is through the major banks, who at regular intervals will draw their requirements from a branch of the Bank of England. Old, torn and worn notes will be collected by the major banks and returned to the Bank for destruction.

4 *Manages the issue of Treasury bills*: The issue of Treasury bills is a weekly feature that takes place every Friday. The purpose of this is to cover the government's short-term borrowing. In return for the Bank acting as 'lender of last resort' to the discount houses, they in their turn will purchase – at a discount – the total amount of Treasury bills on issue. Treasury bills are negotiable instruments with a life of ninety-one days and are issued at a discount, that is for an amount less than the face value. Eventually, they will be sold to banks and other institutions.

5 *Banker to other banks and financial institutions*: All clearing banks maintain accounts for the purpose of interbank settlement. Entries are passed over these accounts for settlement of the Cheque and Credit Clearings, CHAPS and

Town Clearing and the Bankers Automated Clearing. Other accounts are maintained by all banks who by present regulations must have a deposit of 0.5 per cent of their deposits with the Bank of England.

6 *Sterling banker to other central banks and international organizations*: Sterling is still a very important international currency. It is often called a reserve currency. It is important that the central banks of other countries as well as organizations such as the Bank for International Settlement, the IMF, the World Bank, and so on, maintain accounts at the Bank of England for the receipt and payment of funds in sterling.

7 *Lender of last resort to the discount houses*: The discount houses play an important role in the money markets of this country. They act as a buffer between the Bank of England, banks and other financial institutions, so that it is vital they have funds available to meet their commitments. From time to time they may be short of funds. In this case the Bank of England will lend them any sum they may require. They are charged a rate of interest for this service.

8 *Commercial banking*: Although it has been mentioned earlier that the Bank of England does not wish to engage in commercial banking activities, it does, nevertheless, have some customers and consequently, as a very minor part of its operations, does get involved in commercial banking.

9 *Supervision of the banking sector*: Under the Banking Act 1979, the Bank of England has the authority to issue licences to banks and licensed deposit takers to take deposits from customers. They control the activities of all banks by requesting regular returns either weekly, monthly, quarterly or half-yearly. They ensure that there is sufficient cash and liquid assets, capital and reserves, and so on. From time to time, directives are issued to all banks on the policy they should (or must) adopt, or the Bank may issue directives to a particular bank or group of banks.

These directives are usually complied with, whether the other banks agree or not. The Bank of England has the authority to take legal sanctions against any bank that does not comply with its request, but this would be most unusual. Often the Bank will consult with groups of banks before a policy statement is made.

10 *Responsibility for implementation of government policy*: The relationship between the government and the Treasury and the Treasury and the Bank of England is most important for the economic welfare of this country, so when the government, through the Treasury, wish to enforce some political, economic or financial decision, they may use the Bank of England to ensure that it is carried out. The Bank of England can do this in a number of ways:

(i) By issuing directives which will ensure compliance by all banks.
(ii) Call in special deposits. This is not in force at the moment as you have seen from the Bank return, but it could if necessary be brought in again.
(iii) Change the interest rate. By influencing the rate of interest charged to the discount houses, the Bank can eventually affect all interest charged for the borrowing of funds.
(iv) Open-market operations. By purchasing or selling government securities, the Bank may increase the money supply or reduce at will.

Having dealt in some detail with the Bank of England, we will in the next chapter turn our attention to the history of the other banks that have played a major role in the economy of the country.

The business of banking

Self-examination questions

1. Why were priests the original bankers?
2. State the basic function of a bank.
3. What were the reasons for the establishment of the Bank of England?
4. State the conditions that were imposed in the establishment of the Bank of England.
5. Who were the original bankers in England? Why did they assume this role?
6. What were the main items contained in the Bank Charter Act 1844?
7. What do you understand by the term 'fiduciary issue'?
8. State the functions of the Bank of England.
9. State the reasons for the large influx of foreign banks into London in the 1960s.

2 Growth of the major banks

Barclays Bank PLC

This bank began as a one-office bank in Lombard Street in 1692. In the post Second World War years there was a proposal for the merger of Barclays Bank and Lloyds Bank, but this was not recommended by the Monopolies Commission. At that time it would have been the biggest bank in the world and certainly would have dominated UK banking. However, Barclays Bank was permitted to take over a smaller clearing bank named Martins Bank. In 1984 Barclays Bank Ltd, by special Act of Parliament, was allowed to absorb its subsidiary Barclays Bank International Ltd, which was known for many years as Barclays Bank (Dominion, Colonial & Overseas). The amalgamation of Barclays Bank Ltd and Barclays Bank International makes it one of the three largest in the world.

More recently, Barclays Merchant Bank, with Barclays Investment Bank and Barclays Property Investment Management merged with brokers De Zoete Bevan and jobbers Wedd, Durlacher Mordaunt to form Barclays de Zoete Wedd, a major force in securities.

National Westminster Bank PLC

The London & Westminster Bank commenced business in 1834 with two offices: one in the City of London and one in Westminster. Its contemporaries, London & County Bank, Parr's Bank, Stuckey's Bank and others, all established about the same time, due to a variety of amalgamations of smaller banks, came together as London, County & Westminster Bank Ltd in 1911. Later it became known as the Westminster Bank. In 1968 the National Provincial, which had been founded by a timber merchant in Gloucester in 1834 and had grown to become a major bank with a large number of branches in the West Country, was merged with the Westminster Bank to become the National Westminster Bank PLC, having in the meantime taken over the District Bank and Coutts and Co., which were small clearing banks. Coutts & Co., although part of the National Westminster group, still trades under its own name.

Midland Bank PLC

This bank commenced business in 1836 in the Midlands. Again, this was due to a number of amalgamations. Over the course of time the Midland Bank has grown in size. In the postwar period the bank has taken over the Thomas Cook Group – which has large interests in the travel industry and is a major issuer of travellers cheques – and a merchant bank, Samuel Montague & Co. Ltd.

Lloyds Bank PLC

This bank commenced its life as a partnership in Birmingham in 1765. Like the others, it grew steadily by absorbing and amalgamating with other banks.

With the modest beginnings, these banks now control 80 per cent of all UK banking. Nowadays these organizations are not just domestic banks, but conglomerates which have subsidiaries with interests in every financial activity. They all have links to, or own, overseas banks. They are all involved with hire purchase companies, finance houses, merchant banks, international trade, leasing, and factoring, and now, of course, they have major interests in Stock Exchange companies.

British overseas banks

While banks were busy growing from strength to strength in England, there was during the reign of Queen Victoria an expansion in the British Empire. As more overseas territories came under the British influence, so the need grew to provide the expatriates with banking services. They also provided banking services for the local population and facilitated trade between Great Britain and her colonies and the transmission of funds back to London.

These banks – Barclays Bank (Dominion, Colonial & Overseas); Standard Bank of South Africa; Chartered Bank of India, Australia & China; the Hong Kong Banking Corporation; British Bank of the Middle East; Bank of British West Africa; Bank of London & South America, and so on – all with their head offices in London, providing a branch banking network throughout every continent.

Like other banks, there were postwar absorptions. The Standard Bank of South Africa, joined the Chartered Bank of India, Australia & China and the Bank of British West Africa to become the Standard Chartered Bank. This bank has about 2,000 branches in some sixty countries around the world. Barclays Dominion, Colonial & Overseas Bank became Barclays Bank International. As we have said, this name is now an integral part of Barclays Bank PLC. The British Bank of the Middle East is now part of the Hong Kong Bank Group. The Bank of London & South America is now part of the Lloyds Bank PLC group of companies.

These banks had difficulties in many of the countries they served. One by one these countries gained their independence and banking was either nationalized or taken over by local residents. However, their influence remains strong in many countries in Africa, Asia and South America, although they have moved their sphere of operations to Europe and the USA.

Foreign banks

A foreign bank can be classified as any bank which has its head office abroad. Although there were a few foreign banks in London between the wars, the major influx of banks into this country, particularly London, was during the early 1960s. There are now over 400 banks in London at the time of writing. Almost every country has a bank with a fully operational London branch or office, or the very small countries may have a representative office. The major group of banks are from the USA; other important groups are from

Japan, France and West Germany. They give employment to thousands and ensure the continued development of London as a major international financial centre.

Foreign banks began drifting into London at this time because the City of London was the world's leading financial centre. Also, the reserve-currency status of sterling – that is a currency readily obtainable and used for the settlement of international indebtedness – meant that a great deal of international finance was made available through London-based banks. Table 1 charts the growth of foreign banks in London. It is estimated that a new bank came into London about every two weeks.

These foreign banks found London a centre of great financial activity and very profitable, particularly in view of the expansion of the Eurocurrency market and the greater convertibility of the foreign-exchange market, which in brief means that in the Eurocurrency market, money, mainly US dollars, can be borrowed and lent and in the foreign-exchange market currency is purchased and sold.

Foreign banks offer services similar to those of the indigenous banks, but their principal business is to provide a full range of international services to customers requiring finance and advice on international operations (e.g. market research and reports on buyers and sellers). They offer such facilities as factoring, travel services, foreign currency exchange, currency accounts, and so on. Many were, and still are, very aggressive in marketing their services, particularly in the corporate sector, offering loans at competitive rates and gathering funds from the London market without the necessity of opening branches and obtaining funds from customers. Opening branches is a costly business; not only does it mean engaging extra staff, but the overheads involved in maintaining a branch network – no matter how small – are far in excess of the cost of borrowing funds from the money market.

Again, why have all these hundreds of banks chosen London for their overseas activities? The advantages of London as a major financial centre are as follows:

1 A good orderly market.

Table 1 London's Foreign Banking Community

Year	Directly represented*	Indirectly represented†	Total
1967	114	—	114
1968	135	—	135
1969	138	—	138
1970	163	—	163
1971	176	25	201
1972	215	28	243
1973	232	35	267
1974	264	72	336
1975	263	72	335
1976	265	78	343
1977	300	55	355
1978	313	69	382
1979	330	59	389
1980	353	50	403
1981	353	65	418
1982	379	70	449
1983	391	69	460
1984	403	67	470
1985	399	64	463
1986	400	47	447

* Directly represented through a representative office, branch or subsidiary.
† Other banks indirectly represented through a stake in a joint venture or consortium bank.

Source: *The Banker*, November 1986

2 Economic and political stability.
3 Freedom from rigid controls.
4 Skilled, honest staff available.
5 Central time zone.
6 Information technology giving good communications.
7 English is used.
8 Major markets in insurance, commodities, foreign exchange, Eurocurrencies, and so on.
9 Innovative approach to finance.
10 Good profits available.

Merchant banks

When the goldsmiths began to accept monetary deposits, making their receipts transferable and offering loans, they found that this fundamental banking activity was profitable, so they became bankers. Similarly, merchant bankers were originally merchants in London who transported goods by sailing vessels across the oceans, but because they were in a trade centre and they had a good name and reputation, overseas traders kept accounts with them, using bills of exchange to deposit and withdraw funds. Very gradually, these merchants found that banking was more profitable than merchanting, so they too became bankers. The most famous of these is Hambros, who originally were specialists in the Scandinavian trade. Nowadays, merchant banks carry on a great variety of businesses, but each bank tends to specialize in certain activities.

Of course some activities are common to them all. Fundamentally, they all accept deposits and are involved in international trade finance, underwriting and management of funds. Many of them have built up a specialized knowledge of particular markets or areas of world trade. They are the main dealers in the discounting of bills of exchange, and many prefer to be called acceptance houses because of their specialized knowledge and expertise in this field.

In the postwar period they have developed the service of sponsoring the provision of capital to corporate customers. They advise on the best possible time to raise new money in the market, the best possible price available and other important aspects of raising funds by a new issue of capital. They will also assist a company to obtain a full quotation on the stock exchange or, failing that, a quotation on the Unlisted Securities Market (USM). Lately, they have been involved in obtaining funds from individuals who wish to invest in companies approved under the Business Expansion Scheme.

In recent years, any company that wishes to take over another company, or wishes to merge, will seek advice from a merchant bank. A company likely to be taken over will similarly seek the advice of a merchant bank. Also, many individuals who obtain a 'golden handshake' or 'golden handcuffs', or those who have received a large sum of money by any other means, will seek the expertise of a merchant bank in investing these funds for safety, growth or income.

The importance of merchant banks cannot be overemphasized. The major clearing banks realized their importance, so each in its turn has either created its own merchant bank (e.g. Barclays Merchant Bank Ltd) or purchased one (e.g. Midland Bank own Samuel Montagu).

Secondary banks

There are many banks which are not very well known. These banks offer facilities to deposit funds and many of the services available from the major banks. They fall into two distinct categories. The first is that of the overseas bank which offers domestic services via a branch in the High Street of a town or in a major shopping centre. These banks often serve an ethnic community. For example, there are, in various cities in the UK, offices of Allied Irish Bank, Bank of Cyprus, State Bank of India, Sonali Bank and so on. Each of these banks gives a good service to the community.

The second group are what is called licensed deposit takers. They may not necessarily have the word 'bank' or 'banker' in their name, but they are authorized by the Bank of England to accept deposits. There is a very large number of these organizations and it would be impossible, within the scope of this book, to give all the names, but a list of licensed deposit takers is available free from the Bank of England. Each of the companies must state on its letter heading or near its name at its offices, the words 'licensed deposit taker'.

Money shops

These are a recent feature in the financial world. Basically, they look more like shops than banks and are open during shopping hours rather than banking hours. They try to give the impression of having little or no formality in their dealings with members of the public. Their accent is on lending funds for the purchase of consumer durables, but at the same time are willing to accept deposits and offer the basic current-account services, mainly to private customers as opposed to companies.

It remains to be seen whether these quasi banks will be of a permanent nature and build up a reputation and solid customer base. They do attract customers by offering attractive rates of interest, and also attract borrowers who generally are unable to borrow from banks either because they have no account or because they are not good risks.

Two banks need special mention here and are discussed below.

TSB England and Wales

The TSB is a clearing bank which commenced life in its present form by the Trustee Savings Bank Act 1976. Before this time it was a large number of individual banks, each in their own right serving a particular town or small area. In fact, in 1818 there were 465 Trustee Savings Banks. In 1973 many were merged to form seventy-three regional banks, in 1981 these were further consolidated into sixteen banks, with a number of branches each serving a particular area of the country. They still rely to a large extent on deposits from non-corporate customers, but gradually they are expanding their services to include corporate customers. Their range of services include a variety of loans, foreign services, trustcard, unit trusts and many of the services offered by the major clearing banks.

The TSB has undergone a major change. By its aggressive advertising and marketing policy it has expanded its services and has, as described by the Page Report, become the 'third force' in banking. It is a recognized bank under the Banking Act 1979 and a member of the Committee of London and Scottish Clearing Banks. In September 1986 the TSB raised £1.5 billion through the issue of shares to the public and is now a public company quoted on the Stock Exchange.

The National Girobank

This bank was first established in 1968. The factors that led up to its establishment were:

1 The need to modernize the money remittance services of the Post Office.
2 To meet the demand of consumers and individuals to pay bills such as rates, gas, electricity, hire purchase, mail order, and so on, through a giro system, which is particularly appropriate to such transactions.

It is now a public limited company officially known as Girobank PLC and is wholly owned by the Post Office. However, it is still known as the National Girobank.

All the accounts are kept at Bootle, Liverpool, and funds are transferred between one account and another as required. All 20,000 Post Offices in the UK are outlets for the bank, where deposits and withdrawals may be made. The bank is also a member of the Association of Payment Clearing Services (APACS) and so is able to clear cheques through the clearing houses.

Basic foreign services such as travellers cheques, foreign currency as well as remittances abroad are also available. Arrangements can also be made to obtain loans for a variety of purposes, but it is not possible to discuss personal matters with a bank manager as one can with other banks.

Self-examination questions

1 State the names of the 'Big Five' banks.
2 To whom do the British Overseas Banks provide a service?
3 What two money markets in London attracted the foreign banks?
4 State at least four advantages London has as a major financial centre.
5 What is the function of a merchant bank?
6 Describe a 'money shop'.
7 State the factors that led to the formation of the National Girobank.
8 Which bank has been described as the 'Third Force' in banking?

3 Money: the stock in trade of the banks

Money as an asset

Money can be considered an asset, that is something that you have and is of value. It is part of a person's wealth, but it has a characteristic that is different from all other forms of wealth. This characteristic is that it can immediately be exchanged for any other form of wealth, goods or service you may require.

Although many forms of wealth can be transferred or exchanged for other assets, the one most widely used and acceptable in a country is money. This attribute is called *liquidity*. You will hear or read this word over and over again. All this means is that a liquid asset (money) can be exchanged for other goods and/or services without paying a high cost for the priviledge of the transfer. An example of an asset with less than perfect liquidity is shares in a company quoted on the Stock Exchange. If you wish to sell these shares, you must in the first instance telephone a broker to sell on your behalf. You will be required to pay a commission to him for doing so. Having sold these shares, it is quite likely that you will not receive the amount of your original investment – you may receive more or you may receive less. Finally, you will receive settlement of the debt due to you from your stockbroker some two or three weeks later. Money can be converted to other assets with ease, but money will always have the same *nominal* value.

The development of money: barter

In an economy where there is no generally acceptable medium of exchange, individuals engage in a system of barter – the direct exchange of one commodity for another.

The major problem with barter is that of 'double coincidence of wants'. Take for example a Mr Doe who has just made ten loaves of bread. He knows that he and his family can only eat two loaves a day, but wishes to exchange the other eight for a pair of shoes for his son. He knows Mr Heal makes shoes, but lives some ten miles away, and since the journey could not be completed in a day, his loaves would be stale and unexchangeable on arrival. He might therefore exchange the loaves for chickens, if he could find someone to let him have chickens for loaves. He may then go to Mr Heal and exchange these chickens for shoes – if Mr Heal wants chickens. Clearly, this method of trade is time-consuming, costly and risky.

A second problem with barter is one of retention of purchasing power, touched on above. Can Mr Doe's bread be kept? Will bread which is one week old have the same purchasing power as bread which has just come out of the oven? A third problem is one of having a common unit of measurement of value. How many loaves equal three chickens or one pair of shoes? Are they small or large loaves, brown or white bread, and so on? Finally, there is the problem that when, as is possible with barter, there is an agreement to exchange goods at some future date, events could occur that change the value of either commodity, making such contracts very risky.

Early forms of money

History has shown us that in early civilizations commodities, particularly metals, were used as money. Such commodities as salt, horses, sheep, dogs teeth, tobacco, and so on, were all at some time, somewhere, used as media of exchange. In time it was realized that metals – iron, brass and copper and later silver and gold – were superior to other commodities. Although metals served the community well as money, bars of metal were not easy to carry on the person; thus coins were produced, making money portable and easily divisible by weight.

In the market-place, it meant that the trader had two functions: first, to weigh the metal to see that it conformed to current standards; then, if it did, to weigh the goods the customer wished to buy. Obviously the weighing of metal coins was time-consuming, so the size and weight of the coins of the realm were eventually standardized and stamped, as was the case in Roman Britain, with an impression of the emperor's head. England's own coins, which were originally made of silver, were not standardized until the reign of Edward II, when a gold coin bearing his image was struck. It was called a 'sovereign', a name which, of course, exists to this day. Other familiar English coins have names with interesting origins. Guineas were made of gold which was brought back from Guinea, and the florin, minted when silver coins were needed for circulation, was named after the Italian city of Florence.

As the need for coins developed, so pennies, half-pennies and farthings (quarter of a penny) were minted and used.

At this point it should be remembered that the early coinage was worth its stated value in metal content. That is, if you were the holder of a silver or gold coin, then you melted it down, you would be able to receive more or less the same value as the coin itself. Thus the unscrupulous began to trim the edges of coins or, alternatively, made forgeries from debased metal; merchants had to be very wary of the coins they took in exchange for their goods. To defeat the trimming of coins, the London Mint edged silver coins so that any clipping would be immediately noticeable. When coins are debased, and the good circulate with the bad, there is a tendency for people to retain the good coins and pass on the bad. This was noticed by Sir Thomas Gresham, financial adviser to Elizabeth I, to whom the saying 'Bad money drives out good' was attributed.

Recent changes in coinage

With inflation, gold coins were withdrawn from general circulation during the First World War and notes became the standard £1 form of money. By the late 1920s the face value of a silver coin was actually less than the value of its silver content. Very gradually these coins were withdrawn from circulation. Again the copper content of pennies, half-pennies and farthings was worth more than the purchasing value of the coin. Consequently, they were withdrawn from circulation and 'token' coins were issued. Since 1947, no coin in circulation in Britain has had a precious metal content.

In the 1960s the farthing became a worthless coin and no person wished to receive it in change. This was withdrawn from circulation. In 1971 the currency of the UK was decimalized. That is, no longer would twelve pennies (12d) equal one shilling (1s) and twenty shillings equal one pound. Instead, one shilling became 5p, the two-shilling piece became a 10p, while the half-crown, very gradually disappeared from circulation. The old penny and half-penny disappeared and in its place we now have a penny worth the old 2½d and a new half penny. Already the new half penny is no longer acceptable as money, while in 1983 a new coin, a £1 piece, replaced the £1 note. To make money more portable, it is quite likely that a £2 coin will be introduced in the future.

Under the Coinage Act 1971, the coins of this country have legal tender, but up to a limited amount. A person need only accept coins in settlement of a debt as follows:

Up to 20p in bronze (1p and 2p coins)
Up to £5 of 5p and 10p coins
Up to £10 of 20p and 50p coins

Development of paper money

It is probably very difficult for the reader to imagine a time when the ordinary person did not use notes for the purpose of everyday buying and selling. However, it should be remembered that prior to the seventeenth century the vast majority of the population in this country were almost self-sufficient. Their wants were small, travel was difficult and communication outside the village or small town was often unnecessary.

We have already touched upon the origins of paper money, in Chapter 1. Let us now briefly summarize the history of its development.

With the gradual expansion of wealth, more and more merchants needed a safe place to keep their wealth. As we have mentioned, the goldsmiths fulfilled this need. As evidence of the deposits, they issued a receipt, which additionally incorporated a promise to repay the owner on demand. As depositors became more and more confident in the trustworthiness of the goldsmith, the receipts began to circulate, because it was realized that withdrawing a given number of coins from the goldsmith, then taking it to a creditor, who would then deposit it with another goldsmith, was not only time-consuming and cumbersome but also somewhat risky. In due course many of the goldsmiths became full-time bankers, since it was often more profitable than their original profession. The receipts – which were frequently odd amounts – very gradually disappeared and in their place the early bankers issued their own banknotes for regular amounts such as £1, £5 and so on.

With hundreds of banks issuing their own notes, which were of course convertible to gold, a lot of time, energy and effort was devoted to just keeping the various notes separate from each other. Inevitably, inflation was extremely difficult to control in those days. It was the Bank Charter Act 1844 that finally put a stop to the constant issue of bank notes by every bank in the country, although it finally did not happen until eighty years later.

As we have already said, notes were convertible in gold. Even on the present banknote the historic phrase 'I promise to pay the bearer on demand the sum of . . .' can still be seen on the Bank of England notes. Since 1931 these notes have been inconvertible. No longer are you able to obtain the gold equivalent either from the Bank of England or any other bank in exchange for notes.

Functions of money

For any commodity to operate as money it must be widely acceptable to the population of the region or country. Not only must there be a voluntary acceptability, it must also be recognized by the government of the country and have legal acceptability – that is, payment with this commodity is regarded as a legal means of settlement of a debt. To acquire acceptability the commodity must have the following attributes:

1 *Medium of exchange*: To serve as a medium of exchange, people must be willing to give and receive the commodity in

exchange for goods and services. More significantly a medium of exchange allows persons to specialize in particular areas, so that they and the economy can become more efficient. Individuals can specialize in a job or profession that is to them the most advantageous. They will receive money for their labour and in exchange be able to purchase the fruits of other persons labour. With this specialization, the volume of trade increases, the range of services and goods expand and money assumes a greater and greater role in the economy. Specialization is now so far advanced that it is almost impossible for any family to be self-sufficient in a modern economy.

2 *Store of value*: Let us assume that cabbages are money and that we have, say, £1,000's worth. If we hold on to them for any length of time they will go bad and deteriorate in value. But if we sell the total stock for £1,000 we can hold this in a bank without loss. This money can then be used at any time to purchase other goods. Of course, if we wanted to hold the money, we could invest it in an interest-bearing account and so obtain additional funds.

3 *Unit of account*: To act as a unit of account, money must be able to place a specific value on goods and services. Thus it is able to act as a measure to value goods relative to other goods. It is a yardstick which enables persons to compare the relative value of goods and services. In the UK we use the pound for valuing our income and household expenditure. UK businesses use the pound for pricing their goods and calculating their profits and losses. At government level, the pound is used to calculate the national income, government expenditure, and so on.

4 *Standard of deferred payment*: We have mentioned that money acts as a medium of exchange and as a unit of accounting, that its debts are stated in a currency and are settled in that currency. But in modern society contracts are made for settlement at some future date. For example, a national savings certificate, repayable in five years' time, will have a future known value. Contracts made between one

person and another, for completion at some future date, will have to show the amount to be paid or received on conclusion of that contract. Money must therefore act as a standard of deferred payment.

Properties of money

In order to fulfil the functions of money, the commodity must have the following properties.

1 *Portability*: Money should be easy to carry and easy to transfer when purchases are made anywhere in the country. If it is not portable, it cannot be widely used. With inflation, the carrying of large numbers of notes can be a nuisance, so that in due course the authorities will withdraw the notes of lower denomination and issue notes of a higher denomination.

2 *Durability*: Money that does not have durability (e.g. cabbages), will very quickly lose its value. Bank of England notes have a life expectancy of about six months and are quickly replaced by the authorities.

3 *Divisibility*: Money must be capable of being divided into smaller units to allow the purchase of cheaper goods. The value of the sum of each part must equal the whole, for example five 20-pence pieces must equal £1. Some monies in the past have been indivisible, for example live horses – would five one-fifths of a horse be equal to the value of one live horse?

4 *Stability*: Today this is perhaps one of the most important properties of money. With very high inflation, people would not be keen either to hold money or use it. The value of goods could not then be accurately ascertained, and some other commodity would be used as the medium of exchange.

5 *Transferability*: Closely linked with stability is the ability to transfer money easily and without any legal process. It should therefore be easily exchanged for goods and services.

6 *Recognizability*: All units of money must be equal in size, shape, weight, content and easily recognized for what they are and their worth. Often counterfeit money is in circulation, which can make recognition difficult.

Bank deposits as money

Is the balance of your account with a bank to be considered as money? To answer this question let us look at a simple balance sheet of an early bank.

Liabilities (£s)		*Assets (£s)*	
Capital	400	Coins	100
Notes Issued	600	Gold	900
	1,000		1,000

By realizing two facts – (1) that gold in the vaults does not produce any profits and (2) it was not essential for the gold and coins held to cover the notes issued – the early bankers attracted depositors. Thus a balance sheet showing an expansion in business would look like this:

Liabilities (£s)		*Assets (£s)*	
Capital	400	Coin	150
Notes Issued	1,000	Gold	1,500
Deposits	600	Loans	350
	2,000		2,000

The bank is prepared to lend some of its deposits to other customers; for example, a miller may be lent money to buy a horse and cart. The miller will draw on his bank account the amount of the loan, give a cheque to the seller, who will place the cheque in his own bank account, thereby creating a deposit. The bank, then having additional deposits, will lend part of this to another borrower. The bank has thus increased its purchasing power, that is its money.

To continue the example, assume that a note-issuing monopoly has been obtained by the Bank of England, then the balance sheet of an early bank would look something like this:

Liabilities (£s)		Assets (£s)	
Capital	1,000	Coins and Notes	1,500
Deposits	14,000	Investments (short term)	5,500
		Loans	8,000
	15,000		15,000

The bank, continuing its policy of lending money to trustworthy customers, also realizes that as it grows, as it expands its customer base, so it must have funds available to meet demand, and yet it also wants to earn some interest on these funds, rather than leaving them idle. They place their money in short-term investments, which not only give some interest, but can readily be turned into cash if the need arises.

As time progressed, so the amount of notes and coins held by an individual bank was reduced, but funds are held with the Bank of England to meet any interbank indebtedness due to settlements with the various clearing systems. Additionally, the money markets in the UK are now far more sophisticated and banks will place their funds over a variety of short-term investments. Advances also are a far greater percentage of the deposits than they were at the turn of the century.

As you have no doubt ascertained, a bank has the ability to create money almost on a continuous basis. Why don't they? There are over 400 banks in the UK, each one capable of lending large amounts of money to persons in the UK and abroad. What prevents them from doing so?

First, in order to exist as a bank, the institution must have the confidence of its customers to repay any funds on demand. If you drew a cheque in favour of another person and that cheque were returned unpaid, not because you had no funds but because your bank had no funds readily available, you would soon withdraw your balance from that account. Thus all banks now keep sufficient funds either in their tills or with the Bank of England. As an additional safeguard, funds are with the short-term money markets, so that should there be a sudden demand (e.g. in the holiday season or for payment of taxes, etc.) these funds could be returned to the bank if necessary at twenty-four hours' notice.

Second, the bank itself has lent money and in theory most of these advances are repayable on demand. In the theoretical event of the bank having insufficient funds either on hand, with the Bank of England or with the money market, it could call in all or any of its advances to customers. In practice, of course, this would be almost impossible as these funds would be tied up in various assets. Time must be given if a customer is requested to repay an advance. It is hardly likely in these days that a major bank will not keep its house in order and be put in such an embarrassing position. However, if a bank considers that an advance is going bad, or 'hardening', they will for their own protection and for the protection of its customers' funds, call in the advance.

Finally, it is the Bank of England as the agent for the Treasury, who is responsible for the control of money in this country. It has a variety of methods of maintaining discipline in the financial markets and controlling the activities of the banks:

1 It has the authority to issue directives to banks. Thus it may give a bank a lending ceiling, restricting the total amount it may lend (i.e. quantitative controls) or it may tell a bank to whom it may or may not lend (i.e. qualitative controls). For example, it may state that lending should be to those involved in the export trade, farmers, industries in areas of high unemployment, and so on and not to property speculators or for stock-market investment, personal needs, and so on (qualitative controls).

2 The Bank has the authority to increase or decrease interest rates (although it does leave this to market forces), which will affect the base rates of banks and so affect all other rates of interest. By increasing interest rates it should reduce the demand for borrowing and in this way reduce deposits.

3 It may call in special deposits. These are deposits which withdraw a percentage of the deposits, which in reality means the banks have less money to lend. Although there is no special deposit imposition on the banks at the moment, if

conditions exist to warrant such an imposition, the Bank will no doubt do it.

4 The Bank can indulge in open-market operations. All banks hold government securities. They find that this type of investment is (i) risk free, (ii) easy to sell and (iii) profitable. The Bank can, if it wishes, call money in, sell government securities or, alternatively, if it wishes to make more money available, purchase securities from the various banks.

5 The banks have agreed with the Bank of England that 5 per cent of all their eligible liabilities (basically its deposits) will be held with the members of the London Discount Market. This percentage has been static for some time now, but no doubt could be increased or decreased if necessary.

6 From 1972 to about 1974 there was an ongoing bank crisis in which some of the smaller banks had to be either rescued by the major banks under the direction of the Bank of England or left to go into liquidation. Since that time the Bank has insisted that there should be greater supervision of all banks. Nowadays banks must keep a given percentage of its deposits in liquid form – that is funds with the Bank of England and short-term deposits with the money markets and/or government securities. This liquidity percentage is agreed between the individual bank and the Bank of England. The percentage can be increased or decreased after consultation between the two parties.

7 Finally, the Bank of England has the right under the Bank of England Nationalisation Act 1946 and Banking Act 1979 to impose legal sanctions on any bank being out of line, and of course all banks must be authorized by the Bank of England to accept deposits. If the Bank of England wants to get tough, it can withdraw the operating licence of any bank. This last sanction will only be imposed in rare instances.

Other forms of money

So far we have discussed money in terms of notes, coins and bank deposits. However, there are clearly other ways in which we can spend money or settle debts. For example, your employer could give you a book of luncheon vouchers. These are accepted by various eating houses instead of notes and coins and can be considered as 'near money' or 'substitute money'. They do perform the functions of money in a limited area. The same could apply to the large variety of vouchers available either from newspapers, magazines, from packets of soap powders, given to you through the letter box, and so on. All perform some function of money. Other items could include such instruments as travellers cheques, bills of exchange, credit cards and very soon EFT-POS (Electronic Funds Transfer at Point of Sale) cards.

With the expansion of the services of building societies, many of their services themselves can be classified as forms of money. At the further end of the scale, when corporations are dealing with hundreds of thousands of pounds, then instruments such as Treasury bills, and certificates of deposits, are freely interchangeable and can be regarded as a form of money.

From this you can see as society changes, so the definition of money, its forms, uses and functions change.

Self-examination questions

1 What do you understand by 'barter'. What are its major problems?
2 State the early forms of money.
3 What effect does the debasement of coins have on the circulation of money?
4 Describe the effect that inflation is likely to have on notes and coins.
5 Briefly describe the development of paper money.
6 State the functions of money.
7 Describe at least two attributes of money.
8 Why are bank deposits considered as money?
9 Assuming that all customers of a bank require repayment of their balances at any one time, could that bank repay these funds on demand?
10 State the methods open to the Bank of England to control the expansion of money.

4 Who are the customers of banks?

If you start working in a bank, it will become clear to you who your customers are. Everyday a busy branch may have several hundred persons coming through its front doors to do business with your bank. However, not all of those individuals will be making transactions on their own behalf. They may represent their employer, their church group, their spouse or their golf club. The purpose of this chapter is to distinguish between the various types of customer and look at the different considerations which apply when opening each type of account.

Personal customers

These are the individuals who open an account in their own name. Irrespective of their business life or marital status, the bank transacts with its personal customers on an individual basis. As we shall see in the next chapter, the bank must maintain these personal accounts with confidentiality and must always honour the mandate as signed by the customer. Care has to be taken, however, if the individual concerned is under the age of 18, since special legal rules exist for such young people.

So how do you deal with a prospective customer who comes into your bank and wishes to open an account? You will greet this customer with pleasure – it *is* more business for your bank – but banks must take care to ensure that the person is who he or she claims to be and that their 'status' is above reproach. By 'status', the bank is trying to ensure that the potential customer is not, for example, a bankrupt (a person officially in debt with few legal rights to manage his/her own financial affairs). Or, the aspiring customer may be under the age of majority (currently 18 years) and, again, special legal rules apply.

Who are the customers of banks? 37

The usual practice then is to take references, writing to someone nominated by the potential customer for a confidential opinion, and including a specimen signature of the prospective customer. Some banks also take the precaution of writing to the referee's bankers for their view of the suitability of the referee to give a reference. If this seems unnecessarily complex, don't forget that a banker will collect funds for a customer, so that if he collects funds and credits these funds to a person who is not the true owner, he could be negligent. Since a banker is involved in collecting cheques and other monetary instruments every single working day, he obtains protection from the Cheques Act 1957. Any banker who does not bother obtaining references will lose the protection of the Act since this failure will be deemed to be negligent.

In the case of *Ladbroke & Co.* v. *Todd*, the bank concerned opened an account and cleared a cheque for a rogue who had stolen the cheque and then forged an endorsement. The bank could not claim the protection of the Bills of Exchange Act (now Cheques Act 1957, s.4), because they did not take out a reference on the rogue before opening an account for him.

For a new arrival to this country, the banks may request to see the individual's passport to check out his signature and age. Banks are also expected to ascertain the name of their prospective customer's employer, if he or she is employed, and their spouse's employer, if he or she is also employed.

Having observed all the checking procedures and having obtained the customer's wishes as to the type of account he or she wants, how it is to be run and so on, the bank is in a position to open the personal account and to issue a cheque book and paying-in book.

The agreement under which the account operates terminates in the event of the death of the individual. The account should be stopped and usually cheques presented after the bank has been told of the death, may be sent back with 'drawer deceased' written on them. If the customer owes the bank money, the bank has to tell the personal representatives of the amount owed. The personal representatives will take the credit balance once they have the necessary authority.

The bank would also stop an account if they were told that a customer had become mentally incapacitated. This might be a delicate situation for a bank since they are not always able to properly judge the degree of incapacity. However, there is a certification procedure under the Mental Health Act 1959 and this is conclusive evidence of incapacity. The same Act allows a receiver to be appointed (usually a relative) and then the bank can work with the receiver to manage the customer's financial affairs.

The young personal customer

In recent years banks have made a special effort to attract the business of young people. If a young person opens an account, the bank concerned would then hope that they have secured a life-long customer.

The legal rules which govern the banker–customer relationship come from contract law, which takes the view that anyone under 18 years old – known as a minor – may not be held responsible for the payment of goods and services not considered to be necessaries. In particular, the Infant's Relief Act 1874 says that if money is lent to a minor, and the minor refuses to repay the money, the lender cannot take the minor to court in order to enforce payment. Of course, commercial organizations are aware of these rules, which make contracting with a minor somewhat of a risk if credit is given. Your bank would not open a loan account for a minor, without the inclusion in the loan agreement of an indemnity clause. With an indemnity clause (which is put into the contract of guarantee), an adult agrees to take responsibility for the minor's debt. For example, a father or mother may indemnify their offspring, and if the minor overdraws and fails to repay, the parent is answerable to the bank. Have a look at your bank's procedures and forms for a minor's account.

Your bank would like to attract this junior market, yet it must work within the law on lending to minors and on minors' contracts. In the past even the use of a guarantee has not, by itself, overcome this problem. In *Coutts & Co.* v. *Browne-Lecky*, the minor failed to repay a debt and his guarantor could not be made to pay up either, since the guarantee contract was linked to the defective contract between Browne-Lecky Jnr and Coutts Bank. Guarantees do have their uses, though, in adult contracts, and work for minors' loans if the indemnity clause is inserted.

Joint accounts

Two or more adult individuals may wish to pool their financial affairs and open a joint account. A husband and wife, for example, may prefer to use a joint account than to run two personal accounts.

Joint-account holders have different legal rules applied to them than if they were two partners or two trustees. In particular, care must be taken with regard to establishing liability. The law does allow that joint liability exists; this means that if an overdraft exists on a joint account (where all the parties sign cheques), then all the parties to the joint account are responsible in law for ensuring that the debt is cleared. But joint liability has some drawbacks too. For example, if one of the joint-account holders dies, then the bank may pursue only the remaining account holder for the debt, not the dead person's estate. Also, with joint liability there is no right of 'set off'. A manager could not move funds from the individual's personal account to the overdrawn joint account, for example. To overcome these drawbacks the bank's mandate form asks for joint and several liability so that:

1 If one of the joint party dies owing money to the bank, the dead person's estate becomes responsible for the debt.
2 The bank can set off the proceeds in a personal account against the debt in a joint account.
3 The bank can pursue all the parties for the money owing on a joint account until the money is repaid.

The mandate form will also lay down the basis for the legal relationship between the banker and the joint-account holders since it will cover matters such as who can sign cheques and who can deal with other transactions such as the holding of valuables.

The mandate can be altered at a later stage by the parties themselves – one party may stop the other's cheques, for example – or the bank can revoke the mandate if one of the parties dies, becomes bankrupt or suffers from mental incapacity. This is because those three situations usually means closing or 'breaking' the account, in order to retain the liability of all the parties. The death of one of the joint-account holders means that the credit balance can be drawn upon by the survivor. With bankruptcy, the credit balance is divided up between the solvent party and the trustee. With mental incapacity, instructions must be given by the sane party and the receiver. A debit balance means that the deceased (or bankrupt or insane) person's estate retains joint and several liability for the debt.

Business accounts

Your business customers may vary in size and importance from the self-employed 'small man or woman' – the plumber, the hairdresser, and so on – through firms of several people working together, to companies with very large amounts of money flowing in and out of their accounts. In order to know how to deal with the business customer, it is important to understand the legal nature of business organizations. Generally, they fall into one of three types:

1 Sole trader.
2 Partnership.
3 Company.

Sole trader

This is an individual who works for him or herself. To become a sole trader the business person does not have to go through any special procedures. He or she simply starts the business. A feature of this type of business organization is that the owner of the business takes all the risks in return for all the profit. If a bank lends to a sole trader's business and the business fails to repay, a claim can be made against the sole trader's personal assets. Opening a sole-trader's account requires no special procedures (unless the trader is under 18) – just treat this customer as a personal customer. The account may be opened in the business name, and the individual whose business it is will also be identified in the account name.

Partnership

This is two or more individuals (usually up to twenty) who carry on business together with a view to making profit. This type of business organization is often known as a firm and, like the sole trader, the firm has 'unlimited liability'. When it comes to paying off the debts of the business, it may be necessary to call on the personal wealth of any one or all of the partners. Exceptionally, it is possible to have a partnership where one or more partners have limited liability, but this partnership arrangement is rare.

Opening the partnership account requires the bank concerned to obtain instructions signed by *all* the partners as to how and by whom the account is to be conducted. Sometimes partners formalize their relationship in a deed which some banks like to examine. Once a bank has seen the written partnership agreement, the law expects them to conduct the partnership account accordingly. It is usual for banks not to ask for these documents and therefore not be bound by the rules contained therein.

The account must be in the name of the partnership, and the bank requires the address of the business and the names and addresses of each partner.

Like joint-account holders, partners are said to have joint liability, that is each partner has joint responsibility for the debts of the firm along with all the other partners. The authority of partners though is more extensive than that of joint-account holders. One partner, for example, during the usual course of the partnership business, can write cheques which the other partners are bound to honour. Or, if it is a trading partnership, one partner might pledge the firm's credit, and the other partners are bound to go along with this. Clearly, a business person has to choose his partner with care since the action of one partner can bind the others. Many choose the sensible course of laying down the limits of this authority in the partnership deed.

The bank's usual practice with partnership accounts is to

ask the partners to submit to 'joint and several liability'. This would enable the bank to choose who to sue if a partnership fails to pay back money borrowed. It could be any one partner, a few or the whole firm.

Any lender is of course in the position of knowing that after the business assets have been exhausted, the partners' personal wealth may be claimed.

The Partnership Act 1890 says that if one of the partners dies, the partnership is dissolved. The partners may want to carry on using their account during the winding-up process, but if they want to reform the partnership, they must give the bank fresh mandates. If the account is overdrawn, it is broken so that the dead person's estate is still liable for the debt. The same procedure of stopping the account is followed for a bankrupt or mentally incapacitated partner – though in both these instances the firm does not have to dissolve itself, unless the partners agree in their deed of partnership that this is what they would do.

The bankruptcy of the whole partnership is a much more serious business and all accounts must be stopped immediately. The personal accounts of the partners are also stopped and any credit balances in both the firm's and the private accounts of the partners go towards paying the firms debts.

One of the partners may retire and/or be replaced. Again, this would be like a new firm setting up; new agreements have to be signed. If there is an incoming partner, the bank has to see that he or she takes on the debt of the 'old' firm if it is not cleared upon the retirement of one of the partners.

Registered company

The company is a separate legal person in its own right. It can have a bank account in its own name, quite distinct from the bank accounts of its directors, for example. A feature of the company is that the 'owners' of the business are shareholders – that is individuals and others who have bought shares in the company – whereas the business is actually run by directors who may or may not have an ownership interest.

Before a business can call itself a company, it has to go through a legal process known as registration. In order to

Who are the customers of banks? 43

register, the founders of the company have to draw up two documents – the Memorandum of Association and the Articles of Association – and submit these to the Registrar of Companies for approval. These founding documents are the company's constitution and the bank would want to see and retain a copy of these because they set out the powers of the company. The banker should therefore examine these founding documents for a number of reasons:

1 What powers does the company have to borrow money?
2 Can the company give security?
3 What authority do the directors have for giving guarantees?
4 Do the documents (the Articles, for example) say anything about the authority to sign cheques?
5 If this power is not mentioned, the banks would want a special resolution to be drawn up and signed by the directors.
6 Is there an appropriate resolution appointing our bank as the company bankers?

In addition to keeping strictly to the guidelines contained in the documents and the instructions in the mandate, the bank has to satisfy itself that the company is trading within its 'objects clause'. You can find the objects clause in the Memorandum of Association. Known by lawyers as the 'every-damn-thing clause', this part of the document sets out to define what the company was set up to do.

Various common-law cases (though now modified by the Companies Act 1985) makes it difficult to enforce a contract against a company if it acts outside its authorized activities. If the bank makes a loan to a company, for example, for an activity which the company's constitution does not allow for, the bank will find it difficult to enforce the loan against the company.

What to watch out for when looking after company accounts is explained more fully in Chapter 7, on lending. Meanwhile, you should also note that under the Companies Act 1948–85 there are different types of company. The main types of company are those known as private limited companies and those known as public limited companies.

Private limited companies have 'Ltd' after their name and tend to be smaller, often family-run companies. This is because the law does not allow the limited company to sell its shares to the world at large, but only to a small group as defined in the company's constitution. In contrast, the Public Limited Company – the PLC – can sell its shares to any member of the public. This enables the PLC to raise large sums of capital. It is the PLC which most neatly illustrates the split between ownership and control in the company form of business organization. The thousands of shareholders are not in a position to manage the company – that is the job of the directors, who must report on their progress to the shareholders and ask for shareholders' approval for major changes in the company's activities.

Both types of company use the same founding documents – the Memorandum of Association and the Articles of Association. When approved by the Registrar of Companies both are issued with a Certificate of Incorporation. The PLC must also obtain authority to do business, which is given to them after the allotment of shares and without which they cannot make contracts or borrow.

Finally, the members of both types of companies discussed above enjoy what is known as 'limited liability'. Unlimited companies do exist but are rare in practice. Limited liability means that any debts run up by the company are the responsibility of the company (this separate legal entity) itself. If a company could not repay a bank loan, for example, the bank could not normally ask the directors to repay from their personal assets. In practice, the banks may overcome this problem of limited liability by asking for personal guarantees, but you can see that many sole traders and partnerships convert to becoming a company in order to enjoy the feature of limited liability.

Non-business customers

Apart from those personal accounts mentioned earlier, there are many voluntary associations and non-profit organizations, such as local authorities and building societies. Voluntary organizations are those informal groups who meet together around a hobby or sport – the local tennis club or the model aeroplane society are two typical examples. The club will need to run a bank account so that it can safely keep subscriptions paid in by members and pay out for trophies, the hire of halls, refreshments, and so on. It is usual for the voluntary organization to open an account in the club's name, with elected officials of the club – the treasurer or the secretary, for example – being empowered to run the account. Like any other type of organization, the banker keeps a copy of the club rules and will operate the account in accordance with these rules and within the mandate.

The size of the balance on a club account may be relatively small compared to, say, a local authority. Your town hall will be collecting in rates and other sources of income and paying out the costs of the services it provides. The local authority account will be in the council or the Treasurer's name. If it is the latter, it has to be authorized by a resolution of the council.

For building societies, again the banks make sure they have a copy of their founding documents (since, although not companies as such, they can only set themselves up on the approval of the Registrar of Friendly Societies). The accounts must be operated within their rules as well as those defined in the mandate.

Finally, in your working life you may come across individual accounts for persons whose role is defined by law. The trustee in bankruptcy and the personal representative are two such examples. The trustee in bankruptcy is a person appointed to manage the funds of a person declared 'bankrupt', that is his or her liabilities exceed their assets. The account, in the debtor's name, is operated on the debtor's behalf by the trustee. Similarly, companies that cannot meet their debts may have a liquidator to operate a bank account on a similar basis.

The personal representative (who may be an executor or an administrator), is an individual whose job it is to administer a dead person's estate. The personal representative's account, then, is the channel through which the deceased's assets are distributed in accordance with the dead person's wishes, or the law. For these legal persons the banks should always check the authority (usually written) and note any details which will affect the operation of the account.

Types of account

So far in this chapter we have described *who* the account holders are. As yet the *type* of account they may open has not been discussed. What choices are there? The main types of account are explained below.

CURRENT ACCOUNTS

This is perhaps the most common and the most popular account. It is from this account that most services are available and other accounts may be obtained. The customer may pay in any funds he wishes, whether it is in cash form, cheques, dividend or interest warrants, drafts from government departments or, indeed, any other recognized negotiable instrument. The customer may also withdraw funds without formality on demand, usually by drawing a cheque, payable to himself or 'cash' and withdrawing funds from over the bank counter or by the use of a cash dispenser card.

When a person, corporate or not, opens a current account – assuming funds have been cleared and references are satisfactory – he is given free of charge a cheque book, paying-in book, and, at the manager's discretion, a cheque card. Additionally, a statement is sent by the bank to the customer at regular intervals, at least twice a year, free of charge. Most customers who use their current account regularly will request a monthly statement.

Currently, banks will operate a current account free of charge providing it is in credit – that is there is an amount of cleared funds on the account. Any overdraft or payment of cheques against funds which have not finally been cleared will be penalized by a charge against the account. The amount of the debit against the customer's account will depend on (1) the number of items passed during the period, (2) the amount overdrawn and (3) current interest rates.

Before leaving current accounts, a word must be mentioned about statements. Banks must take extreme care before despatching statements since any error, either debit or credit, can involve the bank in a loss. For example, any debit unauthorized by the customer cannot be debited to his account. A cheque bearing a forged signature can never be debited. A cancelled standing order, debited in error, must be refunded. A credit passed in error to a customer's account could also mean a loss to the bank, especially when that customer has in good faith and quite innocently spent the money. In the case of *Lloyds Bank Ltd* v. *Brooks* (1950), Lady Brooks was credited with a series of dividend warrants to which she was not entitled. The bank attempted to recover these funds, but as she acted in good faith and relied upon the balance, she won the case. It is therefore vital for bank staff to ensure that the entries on a statement are correct before a statement is sent out. The statement should be sent to the correct address; otherwise, if the envelope is opened by a stranger, there could be a breach of secrecy.

INTEREST-EARNING CHEQUE ACCOUNTS

Gradually, the smaller banks and some of the larger banks are attracting customers by offering accounts that not only give the normal current-account facilities but will offer interest on the daily balances.

The conditions on this type of account tend to vary from bank to bank, but in general terms a minimum balance of about £2,000 is expected and cheques for not less than £250 may be drawn.

Unlike a normal deposit account, the withdrawal of funds do not need a notice of seven days, or suffer the loss of seven days' interest. This hybrid account is very attractive to customers and so it is expected that as competition grows between banks, the conditions imposed for its maintenance may disappear and all current accounts may eventually attract interest.

DEPOSIT ACCOUNTS

There are various types of deposit account, but basically it is an account that attracts interest on the cleared funds, calculated on a daily basis. Normally, funds that are not needed in a current account are transferred to a deposit account, and a reverse entry is passed when these funds are needed. The individual often uses this type of account as a simple and easy method of putting money aside to meet holiday expenses, Christmas, birthday presents, and so on.

No cheque book is given nor is a cheque card available with this account, but a paying-in book is available if necessary. Statements can be sent at regular intervals. No overdraft is permitted and interest is paid either quarterly or half yearly, depending on the banks policy, but it should be remembered that for individuals, joint accounts, partnerships, trustees and other non-corporate customers, except non-residents, interest is paid net of tax, that is tax is deducted by the bank at the Composite Rate of Tax (CRT). This brings the interest-bearing accounts in line with those of building societies.

Other than the basic deposit account, each bank may offer four or five other types. The first is a form of 'savings account'. Again, each bank will have its own pet name for this type of account, but basically the customer is encouraged to transfer a regular sum each month to this account, and for this he may be offered between 1.0 and 1.5 per cent above the basic rate of interest. The disadvantage is that the bank will only permit withdrawals twice a year. Many customers find this a painless way of saving as it can be arranged that the current account is debited on salary day, so that funds are available for such occasions as Christmas, a deposit for a house, birthdays, and so on.

Amounts of £10,000 and above may be put on a special type of fixed-term deposit account; this attracts a higher rate of interest. Usually, the longer the term, the higher the rate of interest. Such amounts are often dealt with by the treasurer's department at head office. Once the rate and term is fixed, a legally binding contract has been made and it is usual for the funds to be left on the account until maturity. Should the customer require early repayment, then he is penalized.

Another type of deposit account is the savings account for children. In order to attract children, special money boxes are available which can usually be opened at home. The bank would encourage the young customer to come to the branch, however, and credit the account with the contents.

Each bank has its own variety of deposit accounts. Basically, the interest earned on deposits will depend on the length of time, rate of interest appertaining and the amount deposited. These rates are displayed in the banking hall of each branch.

BUDGET ACCOUNTS

This type of account assists the ordinary man and woman to monitor and regulate their cash flow. It helps to avoid periods of shortages of funds with those periods where a surplus of cash is available. Again, each bank has its own name for this type of account, but basically, after consultation with a branch manager or senior clerk, the customer calculates his total domestic expenditure, which includes, rates, gas, electricity, insurance, mortgage, and so on. The total of all expenses plus the bank's charges are divided by twelve, and the customer then signs an instruction to transfer, once a month, an amount from current to budget account. A cheque book is given to the customer who may pay his bills as and when they fall due. Providing all calculations are correct, at the end of the twelve month period, there should be a nil balance, when the whole exercise is started all over again.

LOAN ACCOUNTS

One of the methods by which a bank earns its profit is by lending money to its customers. A loan to an individual may be for the purchase of consumer durables (e.g. washing machines, TVs) or to redecorate the house or flat, or for a holiday, and so on. For a businessman, such an advance may be for the purchase of stock or fixed assets. In both cases the loan may be for a period of two years and upwards. The interest charged will be stated at x per cent above the bank's base rate. The interest calculated is debited either quarterly or half yearly to the current or the loan account at the customer's option.

PERSONAL LOAN ACCOUNTS

This loan is usually for an individual who again wishes to purchase, for example, consumer durables, but in this case he will know precisely the amount he has to pay each week/month to repay the debt. Once the amount lent is known, the bank will add to this an amount for the total interest due for the whole period, and request the customer to pay one twenty-fourth or one thirty-sixth back each month, or whatever repayment is agreed between banker and customer.

Under the Consumer Credit Act 1974, the customer will be informed of the Annual Percentage Rate (APR), the amount of the loan and the amount of the interest added to that loan. Should interest rates move either up or down, this will not affect the loan agreement, so that within the loan time, the customer need not concern himself if rates move upwards, but may feel inclined to either repay the loan earlier or negotiate a new loan if rates move downwards.

The added attraction of this type of loan, from the customer's point of view, is that he may go to a retail outlet, purchase goods for cash or offer a cheque, which may attract a cash discount, which could be sufficient to offset any interest paid.

With this type of account, security is not usually requested by the bank, and with a built-in insurance, should anything happen to the customer, the debt is cancelled and the deceased's family is not encumbered with a debt.

Self-examination questions

1 List the steps that the bank may take before opening an account for an individual.
2 Give at least two reasons why banks ask for references from a new customer.
3 Discuss the precautions that must be adopted when opening an account for a minor.
4 Name three types of business unit.
5 What do you understand by the phrase 'joint and several liability'?
6 Name the documents a banker would need to examine when opening an account for a limited company.
7 What is the difference between a trustee and an executor?
8 How does a current account differ from a deposit account?
9 Why, and in what circumstances, might the bank stop an account?
10 Find out how many company accounts your branch has and compare that number with the number for personal accounts.

5 The banker–customer relationship

The banker–customer relationship is one that has legal obligations on both sides and this chapter is concerned with looking at what those rights and duties are. Before we examine the relationship, however, it is helpful to be clear about what we mean by the words 'banker' and 'customer'.

Perhaps surprisingly, there have been very few legal attempts to say precisely what a bank is. The Bills of Exchange Act 1882 described a bank as 'a body of persons, whether incorporated or not, who carried on the business of banking'. Not perhaps the fullest of definitions! Lord Denning in the *United Dominions Trust* v. *Kirkwood* (1966) attempted to get much closer to defining a bank by concentrating on what a bank actually did – thus a bank was a place where cheques were collected, mandates honoured and loans were granted to a customer. The Banking Act 1979 makes the distinction in financial institutions between banks and licensed deposit takers. To qualify as a bank, certain conditions have to be met concerning the reputation, integrity and sound financial base of the institution. In addition, the institution has to provide a wide range of banking services, such as foreign-exchange facilities, financial advice as well as the two essential services of the provision of current and deposit account, and loan and overdraft facilities.

Since 1979, then, banking status has been bestowed by the Bank of England on institutions that meet the banking criteria. Further explanations on the authorization of institutions to act as banks or licensed deposit takers will be explained more fully in Chapter 11.

The banker is only one-half of the legal relationship. For legal obligations to arise, a customer is needed. Several cases have examined the question of when an individual dealing with the bank becomes a customer in law.

In the case of *Ladbroke & Co.* v. *Todd* (1914) one of the judges thought that a person was entitled to be called a customer of a particular bank after the customer makes a request for an account to be opened and the bank accepts money or a cheque and prepares to open the account. That the relationship can begin prior to the actual opening of the account was confirmed in *Woods* v. *Martins Bank Ltd* (1959), when the bank accepted money with instructions to invest it. The occasional 'one off' transaction for the individual who walks in off the street does not by itself set up the relationship. So an individual becomes a customer not, as you might expect, after a particular length of time, but when both the individual and the bank intend to, and begin to, set up an account.

The emphasis on the intention of the two parties is a governing principle taken from contract law as it applies in any commercial situation. The potential customer makes an offer to the bank to enter into a contract. The bank may accept or reject this offer, but if it does accept (as it would obviously do in most cases), then a binding contract comes into existence, even if the negotiations were conducted verbally and nothing was written down. Of course, all banks like both themselves and their customers to remember what it is they have agreed to do, so the basis of the contracted agreement is the application form signed by the customer.

The banker–customer relationship then is governed by contract law, but the terms of the contract go beyond what is written in the mandate signed by the customer. It is usual in contract law to work on the basis that the express terms (those spelt out either in writing or stated by the parties) are not the sole basis of the contract. Frequently, Parliament, by passing a statute, puts in terms – which are not necessarily spoken or expressly agreed to by the parties, but are included in the contract nevertheless. These are known as implied terms. For example, when you buy food from a shop you are entering into a legally binding relationship known as contract. The express terms of that contract may be no more than the price you agree to pay, and perhaps you describe the goods you want as well. In addition to those terms, the Sale of Goods Act 1979 implies extra conditions into your contract – the food must be fit for eating for example. If the food was not fit, the seller has broken this condition and the contract, and

54 The business of banking

this entitles the buyer to legal remedies such as a refund of money.

In the banking contract that exists between the customer and the bank, the source of implied terms has mainly been that of the courts rather than Parliament. In *Joachimson* v. *Swiss Bank Corporation* (1921), the conditions in the contract were said to be that the banker is bound to:

1 Take in the customer's money and cheques, presenting those cheques for collection.
2 To give back the money on receipt of a written order for payment at the branch where the account is held, or some other agreed place.
3 To give reasonable notice to the customer of closing of an account in credit.

We must also add to the list that:

4 The affairs of the customer must be kept secret.

Similarly, as in any contract, the other party owes obligations too. Thus the customer in a banking contract is bound to:

1 Take reasonable care when drawing cheques so as not to facilitate fraud.
2 Inform the bank immediately if his or her cheque book and/or card goes missing.

Remember, these implied terms are legal obligations, so lets have a look at these obligations in greater detail.

The bank's obligations

HONOURING CHEQUES DRAWN BY THE CUSTOMER

One aspect of the contractual relationship between banker and customer was discussed in the case of *Foley* v. *Hill* (1848). That case established that the two parties are also related by way of being debtor and creditor – the banker usually being the one owing (hence the debtor) the customer/creditor the funds that the customer has deposited at the bank. The situation, of course, is reversed if the current account becomes overdrawn or a loan account is opened, since in both those cases it is the customer who owes the bank money and therefore is the debtor to the bank's creditor.

The bank as a debtor does not have to tell the customer how his or her money is being used, but has merely to pay up when requested. Thus, where the customer is in credit, however, he or she is perfectly entitled to make a written demand for repayment, and providing the cheque is properly drawn, the bank/debtor is obliged to repay the sum demanded. There are some circumstances, though, where a cheque may not be honoured apart from where no funds are available and where the cheque is incorrectly drawn. First, there may be some legal prohibition to payment such as a garnishee order (this is a court order to freeze the customer's account because he owes those funds to a creditor). Other legal proceedings under which it is wise for the bank to withhold payment are those of bankruptcy or winding up proceedings, or in the case of a bank having proof of the customer's mental incapacity and, of course, of knowledge of the death of a customer or a situation where there is knowledge that the cheque is defective in some way. Finally, of course the customer him or herself may countermand the request to make payment. As far as standing-order payments are concerned, these need be honoured only if there are sufficient funds in the account (*Whitehead* v. *National Westminster Bank Ltd* 1982).

Before leaving the debtor–creditor relationship between the banker and his customer, the Joachimson case, which we have just mentioned, also established that in a normal commercial contract between entities it is the responsibility of the debtor to seek out his creditor and pay him the money due. With the banker–customer relationship this is not only impractical but impossible. The customer who keeps a credit balance will have to make a demand on the bank for payment of all or part of his balance. If he wishes to keep his money on his account for a month or year, he may do so. Often accounts have neither a debit or a credit entry for months or even years. In such cases the bank will try to contact the customer to inform him that such a balance exists. Should they be unsuccessful, the balance is transferred to a dormant account, awaiting any claim from the customer himself or from those who can prove that they are entitled to these funds.

Should the bank be the creditor, then by agreement the bank can, if they deem it necessary, call in the loan or overdraft on demand.

MAINTAINING CONFIDENTIALITY

It is part of the contract that the banker keeps the affairs of his customer secret. The bank should not disclose information about the customer's account to anyone other than the customer. In practice, this can cause a bank some difficulty if a request for such information is made. Who would likely to want such information? Well, perhaps your customer's accountant or auditor would want this type of information.

Your bank response would be to seek the permission of the customer concerned, preferably in writing, before any disclosure is made. Sometimes other banks make what is known as a status enquiry about your customer. This sort of confidential report between bankers is a long-established practice and it is considered that implied consent to this disclosure is given by the customer by the action of opening an account. Additional care must be taken, however, when responding to these status enquiries, since the bank runs the risk of being sued by the customer if the statements given are untrue or if they are made negligently. To protect themselves, banks will only give the briefest response, for example 'good for your figures and purpose' or 'well-established limited company who normally meet their engagements'. The replies are not signed and carry a disclaimer clause.

Such actions, in the torts of defamation and negligence, are not based on contract law but are based on the general legal relationship that exists between the two parties.

Sometimes an authority such as the police or the courts may want information about a customer's account. There is an Act of Parliament – the Bankers' Books Evidence Act 1879 (extended by the Banking Act 1979) – which allows for a court order to be drawn up requiring a bank to disclose its business records. Such information could be in the form of paper records, computerized data or microfiche. Additionally, the manager or his deputy may be required to give evidence in a court of law. The bank would not be able to refuse this legal request, providing it was properly drawn up. An order was made under the Act, for example, in the case of *R.* v. *Andover Justices ex p. Rhodes* (1980), whereby a bank had to reveal a husband's account to the police since it was thought to contain the proceeds of his wife's criminal activities. The bank must only disclose the information required to meet the order, and when the bank makes a disclosure under the Act, it is expected to tell the account holder that this information has been given.

Other statutes which give the bank a legal obligation to disclose include the Companies Act 1985, whereby a bank may have to assist an inquiry into the affairs of a company in particular circumstances (e.g. where a member or official of the company is suspected of fraud), and the Taxes Management Act 1970, where the Inland Revenue must be given notice of interest earned on deposit accounts (at the moment, minimum £400) and any other information it is authorized to obtain.

So far, then, we have seen that the duty to maintain secrecy may be waived where the customer actively gives consent (or consent can be implied) or where there is a legal compulsion to disclose. Both of these exemptions were discussed in the leading case on confidentiality, *Tournier* v. *National Provincial and Union Bank of England* (1924). Here the bank concerned had revealed to their customer's employers that they thought he was gambling and they were worried about the extent of his overdraft. This revelation led to the loss of his job. He successfully sued the bank for their breach of contract. The judges discussed two other possible exemptions to the duty to maintain secrecy. They thought that sometimes it might be in the interest of the bank to disclose, and that occasionally it may be in the public interest to disclose. It is easy to think of examples of the latter – suspected subversive activities could mean that the authorities are told. Some writers describe this as being a moral obligation on the part of the bank. As far as disclosure in the bank's interest goes, this is really a practical requirement. If, for example, the bank wishes to enforce a guarantee, then the bank has to let the guarantor know how much is outstanding. The exemption is not meant to be interpreted widely, so if in doubt the safest course of action is to try and obtain consent before any disclosure.

REASONABLE NOTICE

During your career in a bank you may wish to terminate some accounts of customers, perhaps for example those that keep only a very small balance and have not used the account for several years. The law requires that a reasonable notice of termination is given; this usually involves writing to the customer giving notice of your intention – the length of notice depends on the complexity of the individual's account. In *Prosperity Ltd* v. *Lloyds Bank Ltd* (1923) a period of one month's notice was said to be too short because of the consequences for the customer's business.

Of course, the customer may similarly desire to end the relationship. If the customer has an overdraft, the bank is entitled to insist on immediate repayment, unless the bank has agreed otherwise with the customer.

The customer's obligations

TO TAKE REASONABLE CARE

Clearly, if the customer is careless with his or her cheques, it would be unfair to make the bank responsible for any subsequent losses. Since the customer is in a contract with the bank, he or she is required by law not to be careless. In *London Joint Stock Bank Ltd* v. *MacMillan & Arthur* (1918), the customers let their clerk write out cheques which they later signed. The clerk made out a cheque, payable to bearer, for a small sum, but he did not include the amount written in words. His employers signed the cheque, and the dishonest clerk altered the figures to a substantial amount of money, wrote in the words and cashed the cheque. The employers wanted to claim the amount lost from the bank, but the House of Lords decided that the bank was not responsible for the loss. The customer had breached the conditions in the contract that required him to take reasonable care.

TO INFORM THE BANK OF ANY SUSPECTED MISUSE OF AN ACCOUNT

If a customer's cheque book and or card goes missing, then he or she must report that fact to the bank concerned immediately the loss is discovered. The customer is under a duty to act to prevent any possible forgeries or fraudulent use of their account. In *Brown* v. *Westminster Bank Ltd* (1964), a hundred forged cheques had been debited to the customer's account. On many occasions the bank manager had enquired of the customer as to whether the signature was genuine and on each occasion the customer had assured the manager that it was. Thus the customer was not allowed to claim that the bank must bear the loss.

Supply of Goods and Services Act 1982

The banker–customer relationship is based on contract, and in 1982 Parliament passed the above-mentioned Act, which states that contracts for services must be performed with a reasonable level of skill and care. This means that many aspects of the financial services offered to customers – the giving of financial advice, for example – must be carried out competently. In the past, banks have been obliged to respond to specific requests, rather than offer advice when it was not specifically sought out (*Williams & Glyn's Bank Ltd* v. *Barnes* 1980). Assuming that this will still be the case, the bank must deal prudently with actual requests, say, for advice.

They must take care in selecting a reputable broker and pass on that broker's advice accurately. The advice must be up to date and factually correct. Many banks will proffer advice only under a disclaimer of 'without responsibility', although since the passing of the Unfair Contract Terms Act 1979, disclaimers will not always save the bank from the consequences of its advice.

To meet the contractual requirements of the Supply of Goods and Services Act, the bank has to adopt the skill and care that would be expected from a banker, so the bank would not necessarily be liable if the investment it advised turned out badly, providing the advice was not carelessly given. The duty of care regarding financial advice might be more onerous if the customer is dependent on the bank as a sole course of advice – see *Lloyds Bank Ltd* v. *Bundy* (1975) – where a special relationship was said to exist.

The bank has certain obligations under the contract which it must fulfil. In return, the bank may expect:

1 To charge a reasonable commission for its services and to levy interest on loans and overdrafts: What is considered a 'reasonable amount' varies from bank to bank, but is clearly determined by commercial, rather than legal, pressure. The increased competition amongst the banks has led to a greater provision of 'free' banking, that is no charge on a personal current account that is in credit.
2 To claim back from the customer any losses incurred whilst acting on behalf of the customer: Here for example, the bank may reclaim conveyancing fees on land and mortgage transactions or broking fees in investment transactions.
3 To use the customer's money as the bank sees fit: The bank's main obligation is to repay the customer's money on written demand. The bank is not acting as a trustee, so there is no duty to account for the money to the customer.
4 To maintain a lien (or hold) over a customer's securities which were deposited for the purpose of ordinary business: This differs from when securities are left for safe custody, over which a bank has no lien.
5 To expect the customer to be reasonably careful. This applies to keeping his cheque book and card in a safe place, that when drawing cheques there is no room for fraud and ensuring funds are available, or that an agreement has been agreed with the bank for a loan/overdraft.

The customer has a right to:

1 A level of service performed with reasonble skill and care.
2 Confidential treatment.
3 His money repaid on written demand.

Agency law and the banker

As well as the relationship being governed by the rules of contract, there are some circumstances in which the law relating to agency will apply to the transactions between the two parties. A bank will be acting as an agent for the customer in the following circumstances.

1 When it collects cheques on behalf of the customer.
2 When it pays cheques on behalf of the customer.
3 When it buys or sells stocks and shares on behalf of the customer.
4 When it remits funds abroad as requested by the customer.

This list is not exhaustive and you may be able to think of other agency situations in your bank. Legally, an agent is a person (or organization) who is employed by a principal (the customer) for the purpose of bringing that principal into contractual relations with third parties. You can think of it as being where someone acts as a representative of another.

Banks also frequently deal with customers who are themselves agents. For example, partners act as the general agents of the firm, and directors are agents for the company. No special procedures are necessary to appoint the bank (or anyone else) as the customer's agent. An agent can be expressly appointed (by words or in writing) but can also become an agent by implication. So once the bank begins to represent the customer – say, by collecting a cheque – then the bank has become an agent by implication. Similar to implication are the circumstances known as 'agency by estoppel'. Here a person appears to act as a representative or agent and is not allowed to later claim otherwise – as, for example, where a customer always allows her bank statement to be collected by her husband.

It is even possible for the legal relationship of agency to be set up *after* the representative has acted for the principal, or an agency can be created out of an emergency. These are known as 'agency by ratification' and 'agency of necessity', respectively. Only the former is likely to occur in a banking situation.

Exceptionally, a customer may wish to appoint an agent to enter into formal contracts made by deed. Agents acting for principals who enter into specialty contracts need themselves to be appointed by deed. The appointing deed is known as a 'power of attorney'. Banks come across this when an agent produces a power of attorney, giving permission for the holder of the power to do anything that the principal can lawfully do. These documents need to be carefully examined for the extent of the powers that have been delegated, and the bank may insist that its own specially drawn-up form is used. However, for the normal authority given by a customer to allow another person to sign on the account, a third-party mandate form is used.

RIGHTS AND DUTIES OF THE PARTIES

Where an agency relationship exists, the obligations of three parties have to be considered:

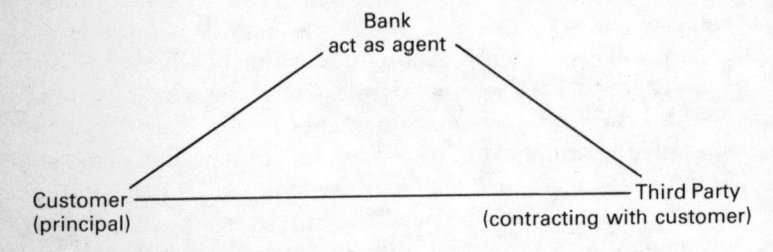

```
                    Bank
                 act as agent

Customer ————————————————————— Third Party
(principal)                    (contracting with customer)
```

Between principal and agent
As you might expect, the principal (your bank customer) is obliged to:

1 Pay the agreed fee or commission.
2 Reimburse the agent for losses incurred on the principal's behalf.

These are similar to the duties upon the customer that arise from the contract between the bank and its customer. The duties on the agent are more extensive. The agent (the bank) must:

1 Exercise appropriate skill and care.
2 Carry out the duties personally. Of course, if the customer consents to further delegation or if the task can only be done by delegation (e.g. buying shares may only be done by a broker), then this obligation is waived.
3 Act in good faith. This requires the bank not to make any hidden profit or bribe from the transaction and to account

for all the financial aspects of the transaction. In addition, the bank must not misuse confidential information and must avoid any conflict of interest in transactions.

Between the agent and the third party
The general rule is that providing the third party knows that the bank is acting on behalf of a named principal, then legal liability rests between the principal and the third party. The banks have to be careful though because they may become personally liable if they exceed their authority and the third party (in all innocence) suffers a loss as a result. Having and understanding clear mandate instructions is important in this context and liability can be avoided if the principal is persuaded to adopt the wayward transaction after the event.

Between the principal and the third party
Where the agent is acting within the scope of his or her authority and the agency relationship is known, the principal is primarily liable to the third party.

PRACTICAL ASPECTS OF AGENCY

For your everyday work it is important to know how the legal rules on agency apply to particular areas of banking practice. Some points to watch out for are detailed below:

1 *Collecting cheques*: The pitfall for a bank here is that should the bank collect a cheque for a customer and the customer has no authority to process the cheque, the bank (as agent) has no authority and this gives the true owner the right to bring an action – an action in conversion against the bank (conversion occurs when the property rights of an owner have been infringed in some way).

2 *Paying cheques*: To remain within the scope of this authority the bank has to rigidly observe the instructions given by the customer on matters such as which signature will be operative on the account. If money is paid out on an insufficient mandate, the bank is best advised to ask the customer to ratify the transaction – since we saw earlier that it

is possible in some circumstances to create an agency by means of ratification.

3 *Buying and selling shares*: Follow the customer's instructions precisely in order to remain within the scope of an agent's authority and be meticulous in recording the financial details of the transactions and passing on the fees. A banker should not act in this capacity if to do so represents some conflict of interest.

Note that a banker acting as agent derives his capacity from that of the principal. It follows then that persons with limited capacity – under 18 years of age, for example – have only a limited authority to delegate.

Safe custody and the banker

Banks offer a service of receiving valuable items on behalf of the customer for safe keeping. Some banks make a separate and specific charge for this service, others provide the service seemingly 'free', but perhaps within the range of normal bank charges. Typically, the valuable items kept in safe deposit boxes might be jewellery and cash. Legal documents such as wills, leases, and so on, may be kept in large sealed envelopes, while many banks will retain stock and share certificates, bonds, and so on, on 'open safe custody', so that should a customer sell a block of shares, then he merely authorizes the despatch of the certificate to himself or a named broker.

Where goods are kept in this way, a contract of bailment is said to exist. The owner of the goods (the bailor) delivers the items to the custodian (the bailee) on the agreement that the items will be secure and that they will be returned to the bailor at the bailor's request. In the contract, banks attempt to limit their liability in the event of loss. They advise their customer to insure against loss. They will also issue a receipt for the box or envelope which will merely state 'Received one box/envelope – contents unknown'.

Leaving aside contract law here, should the bank return the goods to the wrong person, they would be liable in the tort of conversion – as when Miss Langtry's gold jewellery was delivered to a thief who produced a forged release order (*Langtry* v. *Union Bank of London* 1896). Conversion does need the bank to be at fault. The bank may act carefully and honestly, yet if the property rights of the true owner are interfered with, the bank will have to compensate the owner. Of course, if the bank is sloppy and unprofessional and a loss occurs, the owner will succeed in an action for negligence on the basis not of property rights but that the bank has acted in a blameworthy way.

Self-examination questions

1 Which Act of Parliament gives the Bank of England authority to accept or reject the application of an institution to become a recognized bank?
2 What were the obligations of a bank as decided in the case of *Joachimson* v. *Swiss Bank Corporation*.
3 State the circumstances when a bank is permitted to breach the conditions of secrecy in its relationship with a customer.
4 In theory, can a bank request a customer to immediately close his or her account? Give reasons for your answer.
5 State the obligations a customer has towards his bank.
6 State at least *three* relationships between banker and customer.
7 What do you understand by the phrase 'power of attorney'?
8 What do you understand by the phrase 'good faith'?
9 What is the liability of a bank when there is a bailor–bailee relationship?
10 What rights has the bank in its relationship with a customer?

6 Bank services to the customer

Banks are sophisticated business organizations which offer a wide range of financial services to both customers and non-customers alike. The major services offered by a bank to anyone who becomes a customer is that of the safe-keeping of their money. The customer does not have the worry of large sums of cash being left around at home or at the business premises. Add to that the convenience of being able to shop with a cheque book and guarantee card (backed by the bank's collection and payment services), and you can see that it is possible for banks to attract custom by offering the basic services alone.

This chapter is largely concerned with the service of money transfer; that is, how a customer may use the bank in order to use his or her deposits to pay regular bills and so on.

Paying in

Once the customer's account has been opened and the cheque book issued, the customer will wish to keep funds on his or her account. It has been estimated that some 55 per cent of the workforce receive their wages and salaries in a non-cash form. Of these, the biggest proportion have their earnings paid directly into their current account at the bank. Having funds available for these people entails no effort on their part (except not to overspend it). The cash earners, and anyone else who wishes to bank money, can deposit their funds in their account by filling in a paying-in slip.

Books of blank paying-in slips are prepared by the banks for their customers to fill in as and when required. The clerk's job is to ensure that the cash paid in over the counter matches that detailed in the right-hand column. If everything is in order, the slip is stamped with the bank or branch stamp, which contains the date as well, then initialled. The clerk's stamp on the counterfoil acts as a receipt and a record for the customer. Note that it is possible to pay in cheques and other money instruments received from other persons. The clerk would check that the cheque or cheques were made payable to G. Klein (for example). If the cheque was made payable to someone other than G. Klein, then it can be paid into G. Klein's account, providing the original payee has signed on the back. This process of signing on the back is known as endorsement.

As a way of transferring money by means of a paying-in slip, it is not unusual for companies, local authorities and others to issue the debtor with a book of paying-in slips to allow the debtor to go along to his local bank and pay – using either his own cheque or cash to pay money into the account of the creditor named on the paying-in slip. This method is often used by local authorities in settlement of monthly rates, for example, or hire purchase organizations for payment of the monthly debts due, or mail-order organizations for goods purchased. The main services – gas, water, electricity, telephone – will all issue a paying-in slip, usually at the bottom of the bill to allow the person to settle the debt by payment into their account at another bank or branch.

Cheque encashment

We have already seen (Ch. 5) that the bank is under a contract to repay the customer's money when the customer demands it (at the customer's branch and in normal banking hours). The demand has to be in writing, however, and for everyone's convenience the written demand is in the form of a pre-printed cheque that the bank supplies to the customer for this purpose (Fig. 2). There have been instances of the written demand being made in other ways – on the side of a cow is one example! This form of demand would clearly be difficult to process through the clearing system. The customer fills the cheque in; that is he or she:

1 Writes in today's date in the space provided.
2 Writes in 'self' or 'cash' in the 'Pay' space.
3 Fills in the box on the right-hand side with the amount in figures.

68 *The business of banking*

```
                                                  00-01-01
Autobank PLC                                      _____19___
Southtown Branch
1 West Street, Easthampton, ET1 1AA

Pay                                    or order         V
                                       £
                                              G. KLEIN


  ⑈000321⑈   00⑈0101⑈   ⑈12345678⑈
```

Figure 2 *Example of a bank cheque*

4 States the amount in words.
5 Signs below his or her pre-printed name.

This is presented to the counter clerk – the cashier – who has to be satisfied that:

1 The date is correct. In particular, the bank does not want to pay out on a cheque dated some time in the future. The post-dated cheque is risky – the customer could countermand payment in the meantime, go bankrupt or die before the due date for payment.
2 The words and figures of the amount agree. If the two differ, the cashier must ask the customer, if it is the customer presenting the cheque, to make a correction, sign the alteration or make out a fresh cheque and destroy the incorrect one, otherwise payment must be refused. The minimum legal requirement would be to have the amount expressed in words. The bank has to pay on words alone, but not figures alone.
3 The signature is a genuine one (to pay out customer's money on a forged signature is a loss to the bank, unless they can show that the customer aided the forgery).

In *Greenwood* v. *Martins Bank Ltd* (1933), where a husband knew that his wife was forging his signature but did not tell the bank, the customer was estopped from denying the bank's right in debiting his account.

In busy branches it is impossible to either check or know every customer's signature, although in practice an experienced cashier would probably know the signatures of many hundreds of customers. Banks accept that every now and again a forged signature may be read as a genuine one. The risk is a relatively small one, since customers will notify the bank if their cheque book goes missing and their funds stand the risk of being misappropriated.

If the clerk is satisfied that the demand is correctly drawn up, then the cash may be given over. Of course, if there are no funds in the customer's account, or there is an order stopping payment (such as a garnishee order), then the situation is different. Payment could not be made until the orders stopping payment were lifted.

The encashment facility

Customers may want the convenience of being able to cash their cheques at some other branch of the bank or the branch of another bank – perhaps near to where they work, or in the town in which they are holidaying. For the business organization – for example, a retail company with a number of branches – arrangements could be made for the branch shop manager to cash the wages cheque every Thursday or Friday. Construction and building firms, which have men on site, some distance from the head office, can arrange for a foreman or supervisor to encash cheques not only for payment of wages, but for drawing funds for local expenses.

This facility can be arranged for the customer by the account-holding branch who send details of the arrangement such as the cash limit on the facility, the time limit and a specimen of the customer's signature to the appropriate branch or bank. All that is required is a written request for the encashment of cheques – £200 in all for a period of two weeks, £100 per week until further notice, and so on.

If a personal-account customer wants to draw up to £50 only at another branch, the bank would recommend that, instead of the encashment facility, the customer simply uses a cheque backed by a cheque card. Also, if the local bank has a cash dispenser machine, a card will be given to allow the customer to draw funds at any time he or she so wishes.

Parties to a cheque

There are three parties to a cheque: (1) the drawer, (2) the payee and (3) the drawee. The drawee is the person whose bank account the cheque book is printed for. She or he is the person who signs the cheque and is the customer of the bank. In legal terminology, the drawer promises that the cheque will be honoured (or paid) on presentation. The payee is the person to whom the customer's funds are given, or the beneficiary of the cheque. As we have discussed, using a cheque to draw out cash means that the drawer and the payee are one and the same. It is possible to make a cheque payable to bearer, in which case any holder of the cheque is entitled to cash the cheque or pay it in to his account at any bank. Finally, the drawee is the bank who holds the bank account of the drawer.

In the specimen cheque shown earlier (see Fig. 2) the drawer is G. Klein, and the drawee is the Southtown branch of the Autobank PLC. As yet, G. Klein has yet to nominate a payee. The payee could either be himself, or someone to whom he wishes to transfer money.

The paying bank and the collecting bank

We have seen that the customer has access to his money via the use of the cheque. Whilst many customers whose wages and salaries are paid into a bank account, cash cheques regularly, there is also a steady trade in using the cheques to settle a debt, that is the customer asks his bank to pay a shop or the electricity board or the travel agent out of his account. The bank obliges by ensuring that the appropriate debit is made in the customer's account with a credit being made in the recipient's bank account, perhaps in a competitor bank in another town. This is made possible by the clearing system and you will read about that in Chapter 10. Meanwhile, you will note that this type of debt settlement involves two banks acting on behalf of their customers.

THE PAYING BANK

This bank is the bank named on the cheque where the account of the person writing the cheque is held. It is also known as the drawee bank.

THE COLLECTING BANK

This bank takes in the credit for their own account holder whose name is mentioned as 'payee' on the cheque, or if the cheque has been endorsed, then it is evident that the payee has transferred the cheque, presumably for value to the person whose account is being credited.

Stopping payment of a cheque

The request to a bank to make payment can be revoked by the drawer. Providing a cheque has not already been presented for payment and paid by the bank, the customer may ask the bank not to pay the cheque. The customer fills in a bank's pre-printed 'stop' form or writes a letter giving details of the cheque to be stopped.

The bank is not interested in the reasons why a customer wishes to stop the cheque. It may be because he or she has already settled the debt and has been erroneously re-presented with a bill, or it may be that the customer is in dispute with the creditor over the quality of the goods provided. For whatever reason, the bank can comply with the countermand by having the staff look out for the stopped cheque and making an entry in the relevant computer file for the cheque to be automatically rejected.

The details of the stopped cheque that must be given to the bank are:

1 The number of the cheque.
2 The date of the cheque.
3 The name of the payee.
4 The amount of the cheque.
5 Whether it is a crossed cheque.

These details, with the exception of item 5, are self-explanatory. Uncrossed cheques run the risk that the cashier may inadvertently pay out on the cheque in cash across the counter. Customers should know, of course, that crossed cheques drawn under the conditions of a cheque guarantee card cannot be stopped. If the customer indicates that a cheque card was used with a cheque that he or she now wishes to stop, it is the bank's duty to inform the customer, by the quickest possible method, that the cheque must be honoured.

From time to time a payee or beneficiary of a cheque will advise the bank that they have lost or mislaid the cheque and request the bank to stop payment. Under these circumstances, the payee should contact the drawer either by telephone or letter. If this is not possible, then the paying bank has a duty to contact the drawer with a request for authority to stop the cheque. In the event of the cheque being presented for payment after receiving a caution that the cheque has been lost but before contact has been made with the customer, the bank may return the cheque, 'payment stopped by payee, awaiting confirmation by drawer'.

Dishonouring (bouncing) a cheque

The banker's contracted duty to its customer to honour cheques extends only as far as funds are available or any agreement has been made with the bank to overdraw the account up to a stated amount. When a cheque is received by the branch on whom it is drawn, and there is not enough money in the drawer's account to cover the payment or arrangements have been exceeded, the payee's bank must be notified. This needs to be done quickly because the credit to the payee's account will have to be cancelled. The cheque is dishonoured (i.e. returned to the payee's bank) and the reason for the dishonour must be stated on the cheque. In this case, 'refer to drawer' or 'exceeds arrangements' or 'drawn against uncleared effects, please re-present'. The collecting bank may then send the cheque back to its customer with a covering letter advising him that his account is debited with the amount of the cheque. Alternatively, the bank may advise him that the cheque has been unpaid, and his account has been debited, but re-presentation has been made. The payee will no doubt get in touch with the drawer of the cheque, who may, due to an oversight, have not paid in funds to meet the cheque.

In order to protect its customers' reputation, many banks will do their best to contact the customer before returning it unpaid, so that should the customer have cash, it will give him an opportunity to pay funds in. Of course, it may be that when the bank contacts the customer, the bank may be informed that funds have already been paid in at another bank or branch, so that there may be sufficient to meet the cheque, and so save the customer's creditworthiness. Should this situation happen frequently, then the bank would request the customer to agree to an overdraft limit which he should keep to.

If the bank makes a mistake and sends back a cheque which should have been honoured, the bank is not just breaching a contract, but is committing a libel against its customer. It is libellous to make an untrue statement about someone which lowers that person's reputation. For a bank to say (wrongly) 'refer to drawer' about a trader, is to suggest that the trader does not have the funds to meet a cheque. The harm this does to a trader's reputation may have to be compensated for by the bank. It is because of this that banks are so careful before returning a cheque for lack of funds. Inevitably, they will contact the customer first. It could well turn out that money has been paid in and credited to the wrong customer. In this case, the bank not only saves a loss of funds, but its own reputation as well. In 1940 a Mr Davidson was awarded £250 from Barclays Bank for just such a libel. A truthful statement, however, can never be libellous.

The cheque as a negotiable instrument

In addition to being a means of making a demand for funds from a bank account, a cheque is said to be a 'negotiable instrument'. This means that the cheque can be transferred from person to person. For some transfers, the person transferring has to sign (or endorse) the back of the cheque. As such, it is a form of property that can be passed on without all the legal formalities necessary for transferring some other forms of property. The transfer of a car, for example, requires a change in the logbook details, whereas the sale of a house requires a whole legal process (known as conveyancing) to be undergone in order to effect a transfer.

The recipient (or transferee) of the cheque is a type of holder. The holder can often enforce the cheque against previous parties who have signed the cheque. Here is an example. Alan writes out a cheque for £50. Alan is the drawer. The cheque is to pay for goods bought from Brian, a sole trader. Brian is the payee. Brian, by completing a paying-in slip can pay this cheque into his bank account. However, he owes £50 to Carol who recently sold him some stock, so he endorses the cheque, signing the reverse and naming Carol as the transferee or endorsee. Where the transferee is named in this way – that is 'Pay Carol Jones or order' – then signed by Alan, it is said to be a special endorsement. If no person is named, the signature alone is said to be a blank endorsement and the cheque is then payable to bearer. Carol banks the cheque and her bankers present it to Alan's bank for payment. Unfortunately, Alan has discovered a fault in the goods bought from Brian and he has placed a stop on the cheque. What can Carol do? Well, as a holder she is said to have a 'good title'. This means that the cheque has been passed to her without any break in the chain of ownership. As such she has a legal claim against either the drawer, Alan, or the endorser, Brian, for her £50. If the claim was not met, she could resort to suing through the civil courts.

In your bank you may come across very few instances of cheques being 'negotiated on' in this way. The vast majority of cheques go from the drawer to the payee then through the collecting bank to the paying bank. Given the numerous ways in which debts can be settled these days, using a cheque as a negotiable instrument is a rare occurrence. However, it should be remembered that should a payee wish to place a cheque into his account with a building society and not his or her bank account, then by virtue of the fact that a building society is itself a customer of a bank and therefore will place this cheque and others to the credit of its account with the bank, that cheque will need to be endorsed by the payee. One or two building societies for practical purposes do not request their customers to endorse a cheque when paying it in to their account. When this occurs, the building society indemnify the collecting bank against any loss due to lack of endorsement.

Crossings on cheques

Customers may choose two different types of cheques: the 'crossed' cheque or the 'open' cheque. Both are offered with or without the receipt known as the counterfoil.

Crossings are simply two parallel transverse lines across the face of the cheque (Bills of Exchange Act (1882) s. 76). For the convenience of their customers, banks offer cheque books with the pre-printed crossings (see Fig. 2). An open cheque has no pre-printed crossing, although the customer can always cross the cheque himself. A crossing with or without the words 'not negotiable' is called a general crossing.

The crossing is an instruction to the cashier not to pay cash across the counter, but requests that the cheque should be credited to the customer's account. The only time that cash can be paid against a crossed cheque is when the drawer or his known agent presents the cheque himself and requests cash. In this instance, the cheque form does not in fact conform to the definition of a cheque, since under the Bills of Exchange Act a cheque (or bill of exchange) must be payable to a specified person or bearer. A cheque form payable to 'cash' or 'wages' is not in fact a cheque; it is a demand for the drawer to have his own money, which the bank on whom it is drawn must pay providing all else is in order.

The purpose of paying a cheque into a bank account is that of preventing fraud, or if fraud does occur, being able to trace the culprit via the bank's records. In legal terms a cheque which has a crossing can only be paid by the drawee banker to another banker, which means that the cheque must be presented either through a clearing system or by special presentation.

The crossed cheque offers a safe means of money transfer when paying bills or sending a cheque through the post. Sometimes the words '& Co.' are written in the crossing, but these words are not necessary and have no legal or practical significance.

Other phrases used with a general crossing do have significance and meaning for the parties to a cheque. 'Account payee' written in between the two parallel lines, instructs the collecting bank to collect the cheque only for the person named on the cheque. If the bank fails to do this, they may well be acting negligently. However, in practice the cashier may come across a cheque so crossed, and then a decision will have to be made as to whether or not the bank should collect the cheque. Will it be liable for conversion to the true owner? Unfortunately, under these circumstances a collection should be made only if the customer gives the bank a good reason for so doing and the customer's integrity is undoubted. Statute law gives no significance to these words, but in practice the banks have followed the dicta in the case of *House Property Company of London Ltd* v. *London, County & Westminster Bank*, in which it was decided that the bank was liable for conversion for collecting an 'account payee' cheque without query.

The words 'not negotiable' means that the drawer is not guaranteeing the title (i.e. the true ownership) of the cheque to any subsequent parties. These words on a cheque do not in any way restrict the 'transferability', that is, if A made a cheque payable to B, who endorsed it to C, who then endorsed it to D, D's title would be good. It is quite permissible for a cheque crossed 'not negotiable' to be transferred in this way. The only point to be noted is that if the cheque were stolen by X after B had received it, and X in turn transferred it to Y, then Y would have no title to the cheque, because Y obtained it from a thief. There would be a defect in Y's title. His only recourse is to X.

Let us now look at the same situation when the cheque is merely crossed with two parallel lines bearing no phrase whatsoever. B received a cheque which he endorsed, placed it in his drawer ready to pay into his building society account. His drawer is rifled during the night and a thief steals the cheque. By being a plausible person, he gets the local grocer to take the cheque in settlement of goods purchased. If B informs A that the cheque has been lost and A correctly stops the cheque, the grocer still has a legitimate claim on A for the value of the cheque; he has given value for the cheque, received it innocently, and therefore has a good title. Commonly called a 'holder in due course' by Section 55 of the Bills of Exchange Act, the drawer is precluded from denying the holder in due course of his rights.

A special crossing, whereby a bank is named, means that the paying banker has to pay the cheque only to the collecting banker named in the crossing and to no other. Therefore any banker receiving a cheque from a customer bearing the crossing of another banker must not under any circumstances collect that cheque. A special crossing can be with or without the parallel lines, or with or without the words 'not negotiable'. Referring to practice once again. Every bank branch that is regularly taking in cheques for customers will immediately on receipt specially cross the cheque with either a rubber stamp or put the cheque through some stamping machine. In this way, before the cheque is presented for payment it has a special crossing.

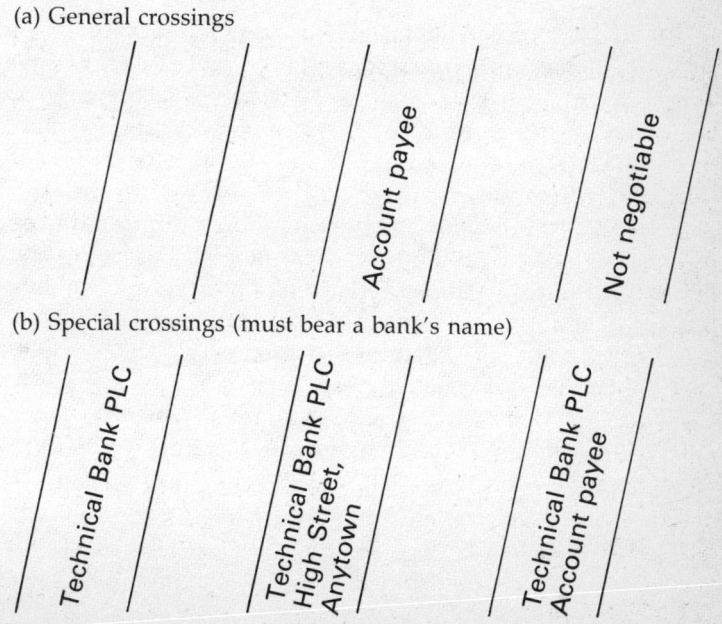

(a) General crossings

(b) Special crossings (must bear a bank's name)

Figure 3 *Different types of cheque crossings*

In the case of non-clearing banks, the Bills of Exchange Act does exempt them. Thus a cheque paid in at the counter of a merchant or foreign bank will bear their crossing stamp as well as the crossing stamp of the clearing bank through whom the cheque will be presented for payment. This is quite acceptable. (See Figure 3).

The definition and purpose of bills of exchange

The bill of exchange, of which a cheque is a particular type, was invented to overcome the movement of gold and silver coins in the settlement of domestic and international debts. It was in Italy in the fourteenth century that these instruments were first used.

Here is an illustration of the use of the bill of exchange to assist in the settlement of a debt. Let us assume that A in London owes B in Brussels £1,000. In his turn, B owes C, who lives in Watford, a similar amount. Then all that is necessary is for B to draw a bill of exchange for £1,000 on A in favour of C.

A example of a bill of exchange is shown in Figure 4. You will notice that in this case the bill is payable in thirty days from date. Bills of exchange can be made payable either on demand or at some future date, which could either be x days from its date or x days after sight. In the latter case, the maturity will commence when the drawee of the bill has accepted it. An acceptance is nothing more than the drawee signing his name with the word 'accepted' on the face of the bill and the date of that acceptance. Should he wish to have the bill paid at an address other than stated on the bill, he would then state as much with the acceptance – for example, accepted at the National Piggy Bank, High Street, Hogstown.

On receipt of the bill by C he would obtain the acceptance of B, then either hold it until maturity or sell the bill (discount it) to a bank for a sum slightly less than face value.

DEFINITION

The definition of a bill of exchange is found in the Bills of Exchange Act 1882 and reads as follows:

Bank services to the customer

A bill of exchange is an unconditional order in writing, addressed by one person to another, signed by the person giving it, requiring the person to whom it is addressed to pay on demand, or at a fixed or determinable future time, a sum certain in money, to or to the order of a specified person or to bearer.

The phraseology of this definition may need some clarification:

1 *An unconditional order*: This means that there must not be any conditions that need completion before payment of the bill, such as, 'When Mr Singh has cleaned all the windows of my house, pay him the sum of . . .' This is quite unacceptable on a bill of exchange. However, where the bill of exchange is in cheque form (i.e. drawn on a banker), an instruction to debit the No. 2 A/c or Investment A/c is acceptable, so is the necessity for the acknowledgement of the cheque by signing a receipt on the back of the cheque. This will occur when the letter 'R' is printed on the front of the cheque.

2 *In writing*: The Act does not specify what is actually meant by writing. Thus a bill of exchange or a cheque can be written on any material that can accept some form of writing fluid. Valid bills or cheques have been written, as we have

```
No. D/987    1st October    19___    For    £1,000.00
At 30 days from date  Pay this  First  of Exchange
_____ to the Order
of  C and Co. Ltd

              One thousand pounds only

Value    received    which place to Account

To  A. & Co. Ltd                for and on behalf of
    84 Hampstead Passage,              B. & Cie.
    London NW1
                                    A. Leclerc
                                A. Leclerc, Directeur.
```

Figure 4 *Example of a bill of exchange*

mentioned, on the side of a cow, others on handkerchiefs, cricket bats, hard-boiled eggs, champagne bottles, and so on. The writing can be in ink, biro, typed, printed or any other permanent form. From time to time a cheque is drawn in some gimmicky form at a charity function. The drawee bank will probably pay the egg, tie, or whatever, but will charge the customer for this unusual service.

3 *Addressed by one person to another*: A bill can be addressed by one person to another person. Either person can be corporate or not. A cheque, being a special type of bill, must be drawn on a bank. A note drawn by one person on himself is not a bill as it does not conform to the definition 'one person to another'.

4 *Requiring the person to whom it is addressed*: The named person is the drawee, and the drawer by drawing the bill guarantees that the drawee will pay, otherwise he is liable.

5 *Pay on demand or at a fixed or determinable future time*: It is important that the exact date of payment can be calculated. 'On demand' is self-explanatory. Presentation must be made as soon as possible on working days during normal working hours. A fixed time could be 'thirty days from date'. The payment of the bill is payable whatever thirty days is from the date of the bill. A determinable future time means that it is possible to calculate the date payable from the date of acceptance by the drawee.

6 *A sum certain in money*: An obvious statement, but way back, before the Bills of Exchange Act, many traders tried to draw bills for loaves of bread, sheafs of wheat, and so on. Nowadays money in the UK is pounds sterling, but with trade and banking being international, money could be considered as any major international currency.

7 *To or to the order of a specified person or to bearer*: A bill that is payable to order must state the name of the payee. It could be 'self' or order, but it cannot be 'cash' or 'wages', as these are not specified persons. A cheque drawn in favour of the latter

two are not by definition cheques, although they are written on a cheque form. They are merely demands by the drawer for his own money.

CURRENT USAGE

Bills of exchange are still used today in international trade. Such bank services as documentary collections, documentary credits, will have the bills of exchange attached to the various commercial documents. All the major banks will also have departments that specialize in the discounting of bills of exchange.

Current uses of a cheque

The cheque is currently the main method of settling debts. The daily total amounts that pass through the clearing systems exceed the amount of money in circulation. The cheque represents a *claim* to money – so that a person receiving a cheque has nothing more in his hands than a piece of paper until payment has eventually been made. So while the use of cheques for everyday purchases has the advantage of allowing a person to carry less money, it has the disadvantage that the shopkeeper may be unwilling to hand over the goods unless he can be assured that payment of the cheque will be met.

Cheque card

A cheque card is intended to give the shopkeeper an assurance that a cheque will cover the amount of the purchases. A cheque card is a bank's guarantee that payment of up to £50 will be made.

All the shopkeeper has to do is to check that the signature on the card matches that of the signature of the cheque and that the (unique) number on the card is noted on the reverse of the cheque. The card must not of course be out of date, and where the card is not a combined cheque and credit card, the code number on the card must be the same as the number on the cheque.

The bank will issue a cheque card to those customers whom it judges can be trusted to have funds available to cover drawn cheques, for example the customer who has a regular income – salary, wages, pension – paid into the account. A cheque book and card together provide the means for the customer to enjoy the convenience of cash-free shopping for items under £50. In addition, a customer can go into any branch of any bank and obtain £50 since the paying bank is assured of reimbursement when the cheque is accompanied by the guarantee card.

Cash-dispenser

Writing out a cheque is no longer the only means by which the customer can draw out his or her money. Increasingly, as technology has progressed and the number of transactions has risen, the banks have looked to automated systems as a way of delivering services. The basic automated teller machines (ATMs) can provide the customer with cash, give the customer a current-account balance, take an order for a new cheque book and an order for a statement. The more sophisticated will allow a customer to pay money in and give him a print out of the account rather than just a balance. All these functions can take place outside the 'traditional' banking hours of between 9.30 am and 3.30 pm.

In addition to the customer convenience that comes from having access to one's funds at any time, ATMs may be used at any location, not just the branch at which the account or encashment facility is held. You can find these ATMs in the walls of the High Street banks. At least one of the commercial banks are building special lobbies to house these machines. The lock on these lobbies operates outside the bank's opening hours and will admit only cardholders, who 'wipe' their ATM card through the electronic lock. These machines are not confined to banks. As long as the machines do not run out of money, they can be located anywhere that is a prime location for customers. ATMs can be found in major shopping centres, in factories, on campus sites of universities, on railway stations, and so on. Given that the machines represent both a capital investment and a running cost, some of the banks have preferred to share provision in order to reduce the cost. For example, the customers of Midland Bank, National Westminster Bank and TSB have all made provision that their customers can use any ATM of any of the three banks.

To use a machine the user has to have a specially issued card on the back of which is a strip. Concealed in this strip is the personal identification number (PIN) of the card-holder. Of course, the card-holder knows, and is expected to memorize, his or her own PIN. The card is fed into the machine, which then throws up a series of instructions (including the punching in of the PIN) which the user has to follow. The machine delivers the money (or the statement) to the user and then returns the card at the end of the transaction. Of course, it is not possible to withdraw limitless amounts of cash from the dispenser. The maximum may be agreed between the bank and the customer at the time of applying for the card, or the limit may be whatever the account holder's credit balance is at the time of the ATM transaction.

A further advance in the use of ATMs has just been introduced by NCR Ltd for companies that have a large number of employees and whose location is some distance from a bank or shopping centre. An ATM owned by the company, with cards issued by the company, can be installed so that a card-holder can obtain funds as required. The machine will record on its computer the amount drawn, the date and the drawer's bank, branch and account number. The company will, at convenient times of the week, withdraw that information then feed it to BACS, who will then proceed to debit the various bank accounts of the user and credit the company in reimbursement of the amounts taken.

Standing orders and direct debits

Any customer may settle his or her debts by the use of a cheque, but if the payments are regular, it may be more convenient, for both debtor and creditor, to use a standing order or a direct debit.

With a standing order the customer authorizes his bank to

make a regular deduction on a specific date to the benefit of a named party. The bank account details of the recipient are given to the paying bank. The authorization can be made on the bank's standard form or may be drawn up on a form provided by the creditor (Fig. 5). It is then up to the customer

STANDING-ORDER MANDATE

To _Bank of Education_

Address _1 High Street, Hometown_

	Bank	Branch Title (not address)	Code Number
Please pay	Everyman's Bank	Newtown	00-00-01
	Beneficiary		Account Number
for the credit of	A&B Insurance Company		7 2 0 3 1 5 2 6
	Amount in figures	Amount in words	
†the sum of	£5-25	Five Pounds 25 only	
	Date and amount of 1st payment		Date and frequency
commencing	1st Sept 1981 £5-25 *now —	and thereafter every	1st Monthly
	Date and amount of last payment		
*until	1st Aug 1996 £5-25		
quoting the reference	6572	and debit my/our account accordingly	

* This instruction cancels any previous order in favour of the beneficiary named above, under this reference
† If the amount of the periodic payments vary they should be incorporated in a schedule overleaf

Special instructions

Signature(s) _Arthur Brown_   Date _20/8/81_

Title and number of account to be debited _ARTHUR BROWN_   1 0 4 7 6 3 7 5

*Delete if not applicable

Note: The Bank will not undertake to
  (i) make any reference to Value Added Tax or pay a stated sum "plus VAT"
  (ii) advise payer's address to beneficiary
  (iii) advise beneficiary of inability to pay
  (iv) request beneficiary's banker to advise beneficiary of receipt.

Figure 5
Source: Banking Education Service

to ensure that there are sufficient funds on the account to meet the standing-order payments. The standing-order facility offers a convenient method for the customer to pay regular debts such as monthly mortgage repayments, weekly subscriptions, quarterly hire purchase or loan instalments, and so on.

The onus on advising the bank of any change of amount or the date of the final payment rests on the customer. Instructions to the bank could be to pay only twelve or twenty-four payments, or pay until further notice.

Direct debits also allow for debts to be settled between two parties banking with different banks and located in separate parts of the country. The direct-debit facility, however, is initiated by the creditor, who uses a debit slip by which the creditor's bank can collect the amount due from the debtor's bank. For example, an insurance company has thousands of customers paying their premiums through their banks regularly. Instead of processing these payments as they dribble in, the insurance company finds it more effective to check them in a large batch.

The debtor, of course, has to agree and authorize his bank or branch to accept these debits – of variable amounts. The debtor will be told when these amounts change. These fluctuations in amount will occur when, say, repayments are linked to interest rates (mortgage repayments) or where inflation or increased costs cause a rise in prices (insurance premiums). The direct debit allows for variations, unlike the standing order, which requires the amount of the payment to be fixed. Some direct debits' authorities are fixed, in which case the debtor's consent is needed every time a change in the amount occurs.

Customers are sometimes unhappy at the thought of authorizing a variable-sum direct debit and the acceptability of the system depends to some extent on the integrity of the participating organizations. In recognition of this the banks require organizations who wish to use the direct-debit system to indemnify the clearing banks against any claims resulting from errors. As a safeguard for the customer, any incorrect debit is repayable without question by the debtor's bank, who will then reclaim these funds from the creditor.

Most direct debits are now produced on magnetic computer tape by the creditor organization's own computer. The direct debit illustrated shows Arthur Brown's authorization for £3.25 to be deducted from his account to the credit of AYZ Ltd (Fig. 6).

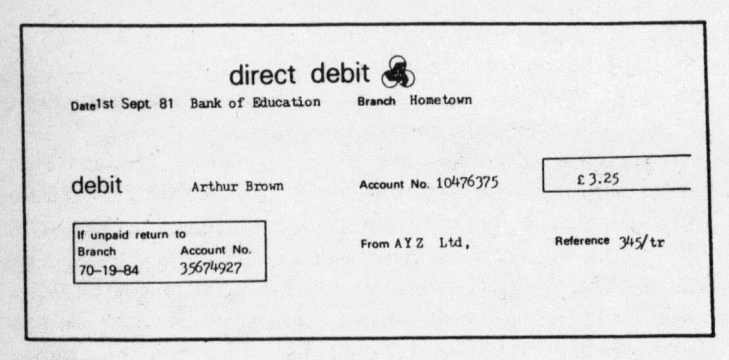

```
                    direct debit
   Date 1st Sept 81  Bank of Education   Branch Hometown

   debit      Arthur Brown      Account No. 10476375    £3.25

   If unpaid return to
   Branch      Account No.      From AYZ Ltd,          Reference 345/tr
   70-19-84    35674927
```

Figure 6
Source: Banking Education Service

Bank giro

Both types of pre-authorized payments mentioned above come under the auspices of the bank giro. This is the name given by the clearing banks to cover their money transfer services. The bank giro also allows for another type of debt settlement – the bank giro credit. Under this scheme a credit slip and cheque are presented at a bank by an account holder. The customer makes the cheque payable to the bank or the beneficiary named on the credit. The customer is saved having to buy money or postal orders and then having to send a covering letter through the post.

The bank puts the slips through the credit clearing system either on date of receipt or, if necessary, on the date instructed. Many large organizations such as the public utilities and local authorities levying rates, attach to their bills partly completed credit transfer slips for ease of use. Even individuals without bank accounts can make use of the bank giro system by making a cash payment over the counter.

The credit transfer system has grown from that of the

traders credits whereby businesses use credit transfer slips to pay large numbers of debts on a specified day, such as wages, salaries, trade creditors, expense creditors, and so on. The non-business customer can deal with several outstanding bills with one cheque using several slips that the banks process in the usual way.

Banker's draft

A banker's draft is a similar document to a cheque, except that instead of the drawer being a customer, the draft is drawn by a branch of a bank on its head office. This reassures the recipient of the draft that the money will be paid since it is a bank that is undertaking to make the payment. A customer might request the use of a banker's draft when very large amounts of money are involved – say, in buying a house or a car. The bank would make a charge for this service. The banker's draft might be particularly useful for settling debts abroad, so it is possible to request a banker's draft in a foreign currency. When a draft is drawn in foreign currency the draft would be drawn either on a branch of the bank in that overseas country or, if no branch is available, on a correspondent.

At this point it should be noted that as well as UK citizens being able to remit funds abroad by banker's draft – if in sterling, on the head office of the bank in the UK, or on an office abroad – overseas citizens can remit funds from their countries to the UK. While all banks in this country are very closely supervised by the Bank of England and we have no exchange controls to prevent money going abroad, this is not necessarily true of all countries. The banker's draft drawn by a licensed deposit taker in the UK would, for all practical purposes, be regarded as good money. However, when banker's drafts are drawn abroad and either payable in this country or abroad, the inexperienced bank clerk should not as a general rule regard all such drafts as good money. There have been occasions when overseas banks have issued drafts when, for example, their own central bank has not given authority for the release of sterling or foreign currency. In this event the payment must be delayed, often for some considerable time. It would be wise in such circumstances to exercise caution and not pay until the funds have been cleared.

Self-examination questions

1 Describe an 'encashment facility'.
2 Define a cheque.
3 State the details you would require from a customer in order to place a stop on a cheque.
4 What do you understand by the term 'negotiability' with reference to cheques.
5 Define a crossing on a cheque. What does it mean?
6 What are the risks to a paying banker when paying cheques.
7 What protection is available to a collecting banker when collecting negotiable instruments.
8 Banks should act 'in good faith and without negligence'. How would you define 'without negligence'?
9 Define a bill of exchange.
10 Differentiate between a standing order and a direct debit.

7 Banks and lending

Lending money is one of the basic functions of a bank. It is the interest earned from loans that brings in most of the revenue to pay the expenses, including staff salaries, of the bank and give a sufficient surplus to pay shareholders a dividend and retain funds in reserve accounts for expansion of the bank.

Before discussing the various forms of loans, it should always be remembered that the funds that are put out on loan belong to customers. It is their money that is put at risk, so that if a bank is continually making bad or unprofitable loans, this will sooner or later be reflected in the deposits. On the other hand, if banks are able to lend sensibly, profitably and, as far as possible, risk free, this will enhance the reputation of the bank and improve its public image.

Before any advance is given, it is necessary for the manager to know the purpose of the loan. The lending officer may wonder whether the loan is for a legal purpose. For example, if a customer wanted to borrow money to buy drugs, would the bank lend money if that customer had no government licence to purchase drugs? The answer would be no. Taking the point a little further. As you have read in Chapter 3, the Bank of England will from time to time issue directives on lending policy. Would a particular loan be contrary to the Bank of England directive? If so, the loan would be refused. Third, the bank itself may have a particular policy on lending, so that instructions will be issued to managers and other officials on amounts, persons, projects, and so on, that they would not lend money on. Lastly, there may be legal constraints on a lending proposition, for example the Consumer Credit Act 1974, and the Companies Act 1985.

Basics of lending

Before any loan is granted, the following questions must be answered by the customer:

1 *How much is required?* This is an obvious question, as the bank must know how much money the customer requires; at the same time the bank must be aware that whatever sum is required, it should not be the total requirement for the project. The customer must be prepared to put some of his own money at risk. The total financial risk must not be the bank's alone.

2 *The purpose of the loan?* As explained earlier, the purpose of the loan must be legal, moral and within the policy of the government and the bank. Additionally, it must not breach legal requirements, such as the Consumer Credit Act. Loans to a company must be within the company's constitution, etc.

3 *Length of time the advance is required?* Obviously, there must be an agreement between the bank and its customer as to how long the money is required and whether the outstanding debt will be repaid monthly, quarterly or whatever.

4 *The source of repayment?* The answer to this question is important to the bank. Any customer must have sufficient resources to repay the bank within the stipulated agreed time – not only the capital, but the interest as well. The sources of repayment could be from wages, salary, dividends, an inheritance, profits, and so on. However, the bank would not look kindly on a loan proposition where the customer stated that repayment would come from his winnings on the Grand National.

Lending facilities

OVERDRAFTS

An overdraft occurs when a customer is permitted by the bank to have a debit balance on current account, up to an agreed amount. Interest is charged at a given percentage above the base rate. Overdrafts are relatively cheap as the interest is calculated on the daily closing balance, which means that when the customer pays in funds the overdrawn balance is reduced, while any withdrawals increases the balance. Agreements to overdraw a current account are usually quite informal, and providing the overdraft does not 'harden' and the customer repays within the agreed time, all is well.

Occasionally, a customer will have an unauthorized overdraft, usually in anticipation of salary day. In this case the overdraft interest is charged at a penal rate. If the matter continues, the bank would request that the customer regularize the position. It should be noted that as well as interest payable on the overdrawn amount, there will be a charge for all items debited to the account.

LOAN ACCOUNTS

Loans are yet another way of lending money. For this method a loan account is opened with a credit to current account and a debit to the loan account. Repayments are usually by regular monthly debits to the current account and credit to the loan account. Interest is charged either quarterly or half-yearly to current account or loan account at the option of the customer.

This method is particularly useful where the customer wishes to make regular payments on the amount borrowed, while from the bank's point of view the monitoring of a loan account is easier than an overdraft. Loans are often given to businesses for the purchase of fixed assets or to an individual for the purchase of consumer durable goods.

PERSONAL LOANS

These are rather similar to loan accounts, with regular payments, with the difference that the interest on the total loan is calculated before the advance is given, then once it has been accepted, the principal and interest is debited to the loan account and the customer repays the total sum by regular instalments. The interest rate is fixed, so that from the customer's point of view any movement in the bank's base rate can be ignored.

No security is required for a personal loan as most banks will incorporate some form of insurance, so that in the event of the customer's death, there will be no charge to his dependants.

Under the Consumer Credit Act, borrowers of sums under £15,000 will be informed of nominal and actual rates of interest.

BUDGET ACCOUNTS

As explained in Chapter 4, this account is for those persons who find difficulty in monitoring their expenditure. It is a form of borrowing and the interest is incorporated in the bank's overall charges.

REVOLVING CREDIT ACCOUNTS

Some banks offer the customer an arrangement in which he or she places a regular amount of money into this account and then has the facility to withdraw, without further authority, up to thirty times the regular credit. Thus a customer who regularly transfers £20 to his revolving credit account may overdraw this account by up to £600. Interest will normally be debited to this account at the appropriate times.

HOME MORTGAGE LOAN ACCOUNTS

Banks, clearers and non-clearers, have entered the home-loans market, which was for very many years the sole province of the building societies. As both large and small banks offer this service, the principles involved will vary between the various banks.

However, as a general rule banks will offer loans for the purchase of houses providing that the loan is (1) not more than two and a half times the individual's gross annual salary, (2) the percentage of the loan is not more than 90 per cent of the purchase price or valuation of the property, whichever is the lower, (3) the terms of repayment are on a monthly basis and total repayment will be made between the ages of 60 and 65 years, although earlier repayment can be agreed.

The monthly repayments will include both capital and interest, and within the agreement the interest charged on the loan will vary according to the changes in the bank's base rate.

As with other bank loans, the bank would expect the borrower to provide a security. Since the loan is specifically for house purchase, it acquires a distinctive character in law. The legal rules concerning lending for house purchase where the property itself is the security, is complex. The loan is called a mortgage, the borrower is the mortgagor and the bank as lender is the mortgagee. The legal complexities recognize that the loan and security are fixed on a person's home. Thus undesirable social consequences would follow if one failure to repay one instalment led to the bank realizing its security by evicting the borrower and selling the property.

Banks, of course, have not entered blindly into the home-loans market. Lending on a mortgage for twenty-five or thirty years is an excellent means of guaranteeing a steady income to the lender, and as security the value of domestic homes has always risen in the long term — since 1945. It is also fairly easy to get an accurate notion of the current market value of the property. Business property is a little more tricky to assess and a professional valuer's services will undoubtedly be needed.

The services of other professionals, such as solicitors, may be employed to create mortgages and to ensure that the bank's interest in the property is properly registered. An insurance policy covering the property (to protect the bank's interest) is usually required and, if necessary, arranged by the bank. The legal, valuation and insurance fees associated with mortgage creation are often passed on to the borrower in the form of adding to the sum borrowed.

If you are involved in mortgage lending in your bank, it will not escape your notice that the procedures seem somewhat involved! This is partly due to the nature of the loan and partly to the system of land-holding that we have in this country. First, there are different types of mortgages (a 'legal' mortgage; an 'equitable' mortgage), which have different implications for the parties.

Second, it is possible for any one piece of property — say a house and a garden – to have more than one mortgage tied to it. Your bank may be the first mortgagee, but this does not stop the occupier raising another loan later also by way of mortgage. It is not unusual for a lender to give a mortgage of say, 90 per cent of the market value of the house. Over the years the house may rise in value by, say, 300 per cent. The occupier may want to borrow money for his business. He can offer the surplus value of his house as security, and a second mortgage over the property is created.

Third, the lending bank will have different procedures to follow according to whether the property is sited on 'registered' or 'unregistered' land. Registered land is where a government scheme for registering ownership or title to land operates. The idea behind the scheme (which started in 1925) is that true ownership (not just being in possession) can be checked against entries in the land register. This makes the buying and selling of property easier. A buyer (and a mortgagee) can tell from the register that he or she is indeed truly buying the land since the occupier is perfectly entitled to sell. The buyer is also made aware of any 'encumbrances' on the land, such as a right of way through his garden, which may affect the land's value. The register is where the bank will make an entry to the effect that it has a mortgage over the property. A subsequent buyer would not go ahead with the purchase until the seller guarantees to 'clear' (i.e. repay) the mortgage so that the entry is then deleted. There are still pockets of land in England and Wales for which there is no registration scheme. This means that the buyer and the mortgagee have to adopt different methods for ensuring that the person selling the house has the right to do that. Title deeds, wills, and so on, going back over time are examined. Hopefully, the investigation will also reveal if there are any encumbrances on the property, particularly those that affect the house's value.

Finally, you may notice from your work on home loans that in English law no one is merely an 'owner'. Technically, a house owner is either a freeholder or a leaseholder. Both types of land-holding have slightly different legal implications. The lesser title is that of leaseholder since ownership is fixed at a number of years. This compares to a freeholding where the owner may keep the property for any length of time. The bank lending on a mortgage has to take account of this difference. It clearly would not give a thirty-year mortgage on a leasehold house where the lease expires after twenty years. This would mean that the property reverts to the person or company who granted the lease after twenty years and the bank would have no security during that last ten years of the mortgage.

The complexities of land dealing have not deterred banks from competing with building societies in the mortgage-lending field. Generally, banks are happy to create a mortgage (using standard forms), investigate title and conduct searches, value the property and set out the terms and conditions of the mortgage accordingly. When there are plenty of depositors' funds this type of secure long-term lending is an attractive proposition. Indeed, recent competition amongst the commercial banks was such that one high street chain was offering to pay all the legal fees associated with transferring the mortgage loan from competitors. The incentive to existing mortgagors was that the high street chain was undercutting the rivals by at least 1 per cent of the interest rate. Given the cost of house purchase, variations downwards in the interest rate are sought out by borrowers.

There are some risks to banks with this type of lending. The risks centre mainly around realizing the security. For a bank to gain possession of the property in the face of continued defaults by the borrower is not that easy without a court order. Gaining a court order is costly and may attract adverse publicity for a bank which may be trying to create a friendly and/or caring image. Even if the property is regained and the bank sells to get back its money, the house market may at that point be in a trough. The fact that in the short run land prices may go down is entirely consistent with the knowledge that property rises in value in the long term. There are also special risks which attach to lending money on a 'matrimonial home', that is a property lived in by a married or common-law couple, both of whom contribute to the purchase price of the property. It is not unusual for this type of property to be 'owned' (i.e. the name appears on the title deeds and the district land registry) by one party only, usually the man. If, unknown to the woman, he offers the house as security for a loan and then does not repay the loan, the bank may find itself unable to sell the property. The courts in many cases on this theme over the past twenty years have determined that ownership can extend beyond the name on a title deed to a joint occupier and contributor. This prevents the bank from claiming vacant possession and cautions them to take great care in lending on a matrimonial home. Both occupying adults should be enjoined on a mortgage deed, or if one party does not wish to do so, they should be pressed to seek legal advice.

Reasons for borrowing

There are very many reasons why individuals, firms and companies borrow money from a bank. These days no matter how competent a person is in looking after his money and anticipating future expenditure, there will always be a time when a loan is necessary to cover some critical period. Here are some, but not necessarily all, of the reasons for loan requirements.

PERSONAL SEASONAL SHORTAGES

Often a person can be short of money to cover a holiday period, or for Christmas or any other major event in the year. Usually such loans will be short as repayment can be from a half-yearly salary bonus or from a profit-sharing bonus, and so on. The money is used before receipt of these additional funds. However, many people find they have a seasonal shortage each month, that is they cannot make their monthly salary stretch a full month. This type of borrowing, often unauthorized, can be troublesome to banks. It takes a little discipline for the person to rectify their spending habits.

BUSINESS TEMPORARY REQUIREMENTS

Businesses usually require funds between seasons, often to pay wages, renew fixtures and fittings, renovate premises, purchase stock for the forthcoming season, and so on. These funds are repaid when the selling season begins, so that the loan is usually short term and relatively safe. Many retail businesses, hotels, travel firms, farms, and so on, are involved in this cycle.

BRIDGING LOANS

A bridging loan is to cover the purchase of a new asset, before the sale of the old one. This usually occurs on changing a business or house. The bank likes to see that a completion date for both purchase and sale are known, so that there the loan is simple, profitable and short term. Open-ended bridging loans – where the customer has purchased a property but has not yet sold his own, can mean that the customer is financially stretched and could be disastrous.

PROBATE LOANS

A probate loan is granted to an executor of a will to pay the inheritance tax so that he may obtain probate (i.e. title to the deceased estate). On providing the bank with evidence of his executorship, the bank will advance the amount required, usually against security of stocks and shares and the deceased accounts. When probate has been granted, and some assets sold, the loan is repaid.

PURCHASE OF CONSUMER DURABLES

This is perhaps the most common type of loan to individuals. The loan is probably for a period from twelve months to thirty-six months. The purpose of such a loan could be for the purchase of such items as cars, washing machines, and furniture.

SUNDRY REASONS

Other than the above, banks are prepared to lend for holidays, wedding receptions, school fees, medical expenses, and so on.

BUSINESS DEVELOPMENT LOANS

The bank is very willing to provide funds for the purchase of fixed assets and stock in order to assist a business to expand. These loans could be for five years and upwards. Security is often required.

BUSINESS START-UP LOANS

Encouraged by government, the banks are giving every assistance to individuals, particularly those who have been made redundant or unemployed, who wish to start a business of their own. Providing the banks can see that the person is reasonably enterprising, willing to work hard and has some knowledge of the business, they are willing to lend on a medium- to long-term basis.

FOREIGN TRADE

Whether a business is big or small, they often look to banks to finance their purchases or to give an advance on their sales. The methods of granting an advance for foreign trade are varied according to the needs of the customer and the risks involved. Often security is involved as the source of repayment is from the ultimate buyer.

Factors that affect a lending proposition

Each bank will have its own procedure for obtaining the information required from a customer and giving him the decision regarding whether the bank would be willing to grant an advance and under what conditions. It is usual for a branch manager to be given a limit for lending with security and a limit for lending without security. Bearing in mind each bank has a different method of operation and each branch will differ with another in size, type of business, and so on, so the lending limits of any branch manager cannot be specified. Branch managers have the discretion to authorize their deputies and senior clerks to lend within a given limit. Any excess must be referred to them. Should a required borrowing be in excess of the manager's limit, then the area office would make the decision. Should the amount be extremely large, then it could go as far as the chief executive of the bank.

CREDIT SCORING

The vast majority of loans are given to individuals. In order to give the customer a quick decision, a system of scoring has been introduced by banks. It requires the customer to complete an application form which asks him or her to not only to show the loan details (e.g. amount, repayment terms, purpose of loans, etc.) but also monthly income and expenditure, marital status, dependants, type of occupation, residential status and other factors.

Each block of information is given a numerical score, which is calculated either by a clerk or by the computer, and from the total score a decision is made whether to accept or reject the application. Mindful of the fact that banks deal with human beings and therefore the completion of a form cannot always reveal all circumstances, the manager has the discretion to overrule the computer or clerical decision.

The credit-scoring method is used mainly for personal loans, and an upper limit for its use is somewhere in the region of £7,000. Requirements for larger amounts or for business purposes are usually discussed with the manager or his deputy.

THE LENDING PROPOSITION

Whenever a customer requires a large advance, the proposition must be put to the manager and he must have a reasonable time to examine the details of the proposal before giving a decision. It surely would be wrong for a customer who has spent weeks, perhaps months, considering a course of action, to expect a manager during an interview to make an instant decision on what could be a complicated matter. The factors that would be considered at all times are given below.

The customer's ability to repay from income
Whether the customer is an individual or a company, this is

the most important aspect of a loan. If the customer cannot repay the loan, the request must be refused, even if adequate security is available.

The customer's character and competence

From the bank's own records, the manager can assess the customer as to his honesty and integrity. The historical records should show whether the customer has repaid any previous loans within the time specified; whether he has kept his promises to the bank; whether he is a competent businessman, always working in an area that he knows and understands. Often persons will venture into a business which they know little about and is speculative. Over-optimism is often found in persons requiring loans.

Involvement

When a person or company borrows money, they must be prepared to risk their own capital and never expect the bank to lend 100 per cent of the required amount. The amount the bank will lend will depend on a variety of factors, but rarely, if at any time, will it lend the total amount. Because a customer is expected to risk his own capital, he is more likely to become involved with the business and ensure its success. Evidence that the customer, either as a sole trader, partner or director of a company, is fully committed to the business must be shown.

Businesses must be prepared to show the final accounts and balance sheet for at least the previous three years. Additionally, they would also be required to show a fund-flow forecast, which sets out the future income, expenditure and profitability. From these statements the manager can more accurately guage whether or not to lend.

Security

As mentioned above, never lend if the customer has no ability to repay, even if the value of the security is greater than the loan. The security is only there as an insurance in case something goes wrong during the lifetime of the loan and the only way the bank can recover the outstanding amount is to call in the security.

The security aspect of an advance should be the last

consideration. Many good loans are given after an informal discussion with the customer – perhaps over the telephone – and no security is requested nor offered. Having said that, it is regretted that many loans are given with security as the major consideration.

Security can come from the person himself or can come from a third party. Such items as stocks and shares, property, life policies, guarantees, documents of title, are given either by the customer or a third party as security for a loan. Providing the bank can find the value of the security, obtain good title and that it is marketable without undue problems, then it will readily take what is offered.

Lending to companies

As we have already seen in Chapter 4, a company is a separate legal entity. That is, it is responsible for its own debts and the members of that company cannot be made liable and sued for any outstanding monies owed. Therefore a bank that lends money to a company must take additional precautions for any advances given.

First, it will ensure that the project for which the money is required is within the objects of the company; that is, the terms of the company's existence as stated in the Memorandum of Association must cover the operations for which the money is required.

Second, the bank must ensure that the company has the power to borrow, as stated within the Memorandum of Association, and additionally, that the Articles of Association give the directors borrowing authority. It is for this reason that the bank, when opening an account for a limited company, retains a copy of the Memorandum and Articles of Association.

The third precaution is a copy of the minute of the directors' meeting authorizing an approach to the bank for the sum required and confirming that the borrowing is within the terms of the Memorandum and Articles of Association. After all, it is quite possible that an amendment to the Memorandum and Articles of Association has been made without the knowledge of the bank, so the bank must clear itself for this purpose.

Finally, the bank would like to see the audited accounts and balance sheet of the company for at least three years and, wherever possible, a fund-flow forecast showing how the company intends to utilize the funds and the future profitability of the company, which of course will show the source of repayment of the borrowing and the interest due. Should the borrowing be four, five or six months from the date of the last balance sheet, it would be expected that up-to-date figures would be given to enable the bank to produce final accounts and a 'statement of affairs', which is basically the same as a balance sheet, so that the manager has a clearer understanding of the current financial situation of the borrowing company.

LEGAL CONSIDERATIONS

Perhaps the most important piece of legislation to affect bank lending is the Consumer Credit Act 1974. Passed more than ten years ago, it is only recently that all provisions of the Act have been brought into force. Broadly speaking, the purpose of the Act is to ensure that consumers or borrowers are fully aware of their rights and obligations under the loan agreement. The cost of protecting the consumer falls largely on the lender, who is now faced with having to conform to the exacting demands of the legislation. Since the Act is designed to protect individuals, lending to limited companies is exempt from the provisions, as is lending for finance of foreign trade and loans for more than £15,000. Note that this monetary limit is raised from time to time. Bridging loans are often exempt (if repayable in four instalments or less) and so are certain loans for insurance policies.

So what requirements do the banks have to meet? The main requirement is that the act of granting credit of up to £15,000 to an individual (whether a sole trader, a joint-account holder, a partner, executor, trustee or member of an unincorporated club) is known under the Act as a *regulated agreement* and a regulated agreement must be in writing. The only exemption from this rule is when the loan is made via an overdraft. The idea is that the consumer/borrower is more likely to appreciate that he or she is entering into a legally binding agreement if the loan is set out in a formal manner. Of course, banks have always been keen to have accurate records of agreements and have on the whole put loan agreements into writing. Now, their standard forms must make the distinction between regulated and non-regulated agreements, and the former must follow the exacting guidelines in the Act. The prescribed format, for example, must include the cost of borrowing expressed as an annual percentage rate and the total charge for the credit; the form must be headed up as a regulated agreement governed by the Consumer Credit Act and must be signed by both parties; there must be clear statements (in an approved form) of protections and remedies available to the consumer, such as the right to cancel.

Apart from setting up the regulated loan in the proper manner, the Act places other obligations on the lending party. There are some strict rules about canvassing for lending, so that a bank manager is not allowed to solicit for loan business from an individual away from the bank premises without the individual's prior invitation. Even a customer's business premises would prohibit an unsolicited invitation to borrow money – unless the invitation concerned an overdraft for an existing customer, since overdraft facilities can be canvassed for. There are special rules that prohibit canvassing a minor in an attempt to increase lending, and provisions regarding advertising generally. Any request from a customer, however, about outstanding borrowing under a regulated agreement must be responded to. Statements must be provided at least once every twelve months or when a charge has been made. Joint-account holders are entitled to separate statements unless they agree (by signing a statement) to dispense with one copy.

Protection extends to the customer to the extent that if the loan agreement is signed away from the bank premises, there is a 'cooling off' period built into the agreement by the Act. This means that if the borrower changes his or her mind shortly after signing, he or she can withdraw from the contract without any legal or financial repercussions. If the agreement is signed at the bank, it is a non-cancellable agreement – just like any other contract, it is discharged only when both parties have fulfilled their obligations. If the customer defaults on the loan, there is a special procedure to be followed.

The Consumer Credit Act, then, attempts to safeguard consumer rights by:

1 Requiring regulated agreements in writing, signed by the parties and in a prescribed format.
2 Obliging the lender to provide certain information for the borrower.
3 Including cancellation rights and default procedures in certain types of regulated agreements.
4 In the final resort, empowering the courts to rewrite agreements if they consider the loan to be an 'extortionate credit bargain'. However, this is not likely to be used against banks, whose cost of borrowing is competitive.

Whilst banks have on the whole been seen to act with integrity, there was evidence prior to the passing of the Consumer Credit Act (and its predecessors, the Hire Purchase Acts) of many flagrant abuses in the relationship of borrower and lender. The lender frequently relied on overpersuasive selling methods of expensive credit, attracting gullible borrowers who did not appreciate that they were committed by contract to continue the relationship. Hopefully, the provisions of the Act will stop the 'cowboy' credit brokers and educate the consumer into better money management. Some lending institutions will henceforward require a licence and the licence can be revoked if the giver of credit flouts the Act and its regulations.

Meanwhile, the banks are having to interpret the provisions of the Act, without benefit of case law, in order to avoid possibly committing a criminal offence or ending up with an unenforceable agreement. The banks have the aid of guidelines issued by the Office of Fair Trading and, given the very wide application of the Act (securities, guarantees, credit cards, etc. – are all affected), these are very important indeed.

CONCLUSION

As you can now see, lending is a highly skilled operation and only undertaken by senior clerks, supervisors and managers.

Training is given by a bank to clerks to whom they wish to give responsibility for this function. The bank's own principles and procedures are fully explained. Many bank training centres use mneumonic words to assist the clerk to understand and arrive at a correct answer. The following words are frequently used by loan clerks to cover the various aspects of a loan:

CAMPARI: Character of customer
Amount
Means
Purpose
Accountability
Risks
Insurance (security)

PARSAR: Purpose
Amount
Reason
Source of repayment/security
Ability
Risks

Credit cards

Although the lending function is a major service of a bank, you are probably aware that all banks have ownership or part ownership of a credit card company. For example, Barclays Bank own Barclaycard, part of Visa card; TSB, have their Trustcard, also part of Visa; while Lloyds, Midland and National Westminster and Royal Bank of Scotland have a share in Access.

Credit cards are plastic cards issued to persons, not necessarily customers of a bank, which have on the front, the person's name, credit card number, date of expiry. On the reverse of the card is the signature of the holder and the basic conditions of issue. It should be remembered at all times that this card is the property of the credit card company.

In order to obtain a card, a person must complete a form which contains his name, address, marital status, employment and salary details and many other facts so that the credit card company may assess his or her creditworthiness and the limit of credit that should be given. Once a card has been issued, the holder may use it (1) to withdraw funds from a bank either over the counter or from a cash dispenser or (2) to purchase goods and services from any retail outlet.

When the customer obtains funds from a bank he may do so up to the limit stipulated. This is regarded as a loan which not only attracts a handling charge, but interest at the current rate, which at the time of writing is somewhere in the region of 2 per cent per month or between about 25 and 30 per cent per annum. The rate is often far greater than a loan or overdraft.

However, with a credit card used for the purchase of goods and services, it is possible to obtain up to about six weeks' credit, interest free. For example, when purchasing goods at the beginning of a month and paying for them by credit card, it is quite likely that settlement need not be made until the middle of the following month. This interest-free credit is very attractive to persons who have got the discipline to control their spending and pay their bills as and when they fall due.

Not only can the credit card be used in shops, supermarkets, and so on, but in hotels and restaurants and when ordering goods by mail order. The card can also be used abroad; in fact the co-author used his card quite extensively while on holiday in Europe and it was over two months before the amounts appeared on the statement – very useful extended free credit.

The credit card companies obtain their profits from two basic sources:

1 Interest from credit card holders who do not pay the amount due to the date specified.
2 A charge to the retailer of between 2.5 and 5 per cent on the turnover. That is, if a retailer presents vouchers to a bank for credit to his account for £10,000 and the agreement is a commission of 5 per cent, then the credit card company will

at the end of the month pass a direct debit for £500 to the retailer's current amount.

In addition to the normal credit card, many banks are issuing cards which indicate a higher financial status and automatically gives the holder a greater amount of credit, additional insurance and other factors. These concessions will vary slightly from bank to bank.

Very many persons use the credit card as a means of obtaining credit. Whether this is an acceptable way of borrowing is a subjective decision. Generally speaking, it seems that it is easier to obtain funds from a credit card company than from a bank. This is evident from the poor publicity through the media, which seems to indicate that the credit card companies often lend money to those who can least afford to repay.

Self-examination questions

1 State the main source of funds that enable banks to lend money.
2 State the four basic questions that must be answered satisfactorily before an advance is granted.
3 Describe how a loan account differs from a personal loan account.
4 When a bank lends money for a home mortgage, what other professional services are required before final completion of the contract?
5 In what ways does a freeholder differ from a leaseholder?
6 Describe a probate loan?
7 Describe how your bank undertakes credit scoring?
8 Name three items that are acceptable to a bank as security.
9 What is the purpose of the Consumer Credit Act 1974?
10 What do you understand by the term 'regulated agreement'?

8 Domestic services of banks

The phenomenal growth of financial services other than the traditional banking services of deposit taking, lending and money transmission, is a comparatively recent one. In the last two decades banks have diversified into associated financial fields which up to then were barely, if at all, connected to banking. As competition between all financial institutions has increased, so has the pressure of each bank to offer a comprehensive 'one stop' banking so that each customer's financial needs can be met by his or her banker.

Some services are obvious offshoots of 'traditional' banking. If it was part of a bank's function to take deposits (*UDT* v. *Kirkwood*), then one aspect of this function would be the provision of night-safe facilities.

Night-safe facilities

Aimed at the business customer who needed a secure place for the day's takings, a night safe enables cash to be deposited after the bank has closed. The sole trader is given a leather wallet which he or she can fill with the money then lock. The leather wallet is then posted into the wall safe, which itself can only be opened with a key given to the night-safe customers. The wall-safe deposits the wallets at the bottom of a shute. In the morning the bank staff clear the safe and record the contents in the record book. Some wallets are then emptied by the bank staff and the proceeds deposited to the credit of the customer's account. The customer can opt for a different type of wallet whereby the bank staff do not open the wallet but retain it for returning intact to the customer, who collects it during the day. It is then up to the customer whether all or part of the cash is banked. This type of facility meets the needs of business people who accumulate cash during the day and whose business closes outside banking hours. They are relieved of the worry of keeping large amounts of cash at their business or at their homes.

Safe custody

A similar service is that of safe custody. Again perceived as being close to the traditional role of the bank, safe-custody services have existed a long time.

This service offers customers the opportunity to leave their valuables in a safe place, that is in the strong rooms of banks. The contents of the locked box (or sealed envelope) are not known to the safe keeper. The customer places the items (e.g. jewellery or documents) into the box or envelope and then seals or locks the container before handing it to a member of the bank staff. The bank acknowledges receipt of the container and advises the customer to insure against loss for any items deposited.

'Break-ins' into strong rooms are exceedingly rare, yet worth insuring against. The bank discharges its duty as a keeper of the goods (a bailee) by ensuring that the property is returned only in accordance with the mandate. To do otherwise leaves the bank liable to be sued for conversion. The bank would be failing in its duty as bailee if the bank staff were careless with the property in any way – if doors that were meant to be locked were left unlocked, for example, and a sneak theft occurred. The customer whose property was lost would have an action in negligence against the bank for the careless actions of its staff.

In addition to offering to retain a sealed envelope or a box, the bank will also offer facilities of 'open-safe custody'. This is when a customer who buys and sells shares asks the bank to retain the certificates in the strong room on a shelf, so that should he decide to sell any of his investments, he does not have to collect his envelope or box, but authority can be given to remit the appropriate certificate direct to the broker. The same system could apply to building society pass books, national savings books, and so on.

The bank has the right to refuse to accept an item in safe custody. For example, if a person were going abroad for a number of years, then to place a very large container which held his suits and other clothing would not be acceptable. Nor, in fact, would valuable paintings, if the manager considered that they could be damaged due to lack of proper ventilation. With the awareness of strict security in banks, again the bank must be sure of the integrity of the customer before accepting any box, container or envelope.

Safe deposit

Some banks prefer to offer this service, as the customer can enter the strong room, during normal business hours, and alter the contents of his or her box. The customer alone has the key to the box, although in case of emergency the bank can have a duplicate, which would not normally be used except in the presence of the customer or by his or her express authority.

Investment services

A development of the traditional role of the banker is the banks' entry into the field of investment services.

Banks have traditionally encouraged savings, via deposits, and of course utilized these deposits in their own investments. It is a comparatively new step for banks to be involved with how customers put their own capital funds to work. It is not any longer thought desirable for bank managers to be 'financial advisers' *per se*. In particular, banks are sensitive to a possible claim by the customer in negligence, if the investment turns out badly. Indeed, if they represent themselves as being available to give professional advice and they fail to give a reasonable standard of service, aggrieved customers may well have a claim in negligence (*Woods* v. *Martins Bank Ltd*, see Appendix I, p. 213).

Banks prefer the manager's role to be that of a channel between a professional adviser, such as a stockbroker, and a customer. Thus for most banks, where the customer asks for advice, the investment service consists of passing on, accurately, the comments of one of the stockbrokers allocated to the branch or that of its own investment advisers, depending on the need of the customer.

The most common form of service is that of the use of the stockbroker. In this case the bank supplies the broker with the details of the customer's financial background, which could include age, occupation, tax position, need for capital or income, or indeed any information that could be relevant to an investment decision. In the past the banks have transmitted the broker's response to the customer with a disclaimer as to their own responsibility. Since the passing of the Unfair Contract Terms Act 1979, the use of limitation clauses or disclaimers is less certain. It may well be that in a case in court, a bank will not necessarily benefit from the use of a disclaimer. In the final analysis, the choice of investment is left to the customer to determine from the options outlined by the broker.

STOCKS AND SHARES

Requests to the branch manager for the purchase of particular stocks or shares pose no problem. The customer's instructions are telephoned to the stockbroker and then confirmed in writing. The bank's responsibility here is to transmit the order accurately, having selected a broker of good repute. The charge for the service is borne not by the customer but the broker, who agrees to pass on 25 per cent of the commission received from the customer to the bank. Eventually, the certificate is received from the broker and the bank will either send this certificate to the customer or, if instructions have been received, retain it on his behalf in safe custody.

Part of a bank's investment services may be that of managing a portfolio on behalf of customers. This is a service taken up by individuals working abroad or simply those that dislike the bother of attending to rights issues or dealing with dividend warrants themselves. The investments are transferred to the bank's name or that of their nominee company, and thereafter the bank collects the dividends and interest, and credits the customer's account. As an aid to the customer, the bank will maintain a valuation of the portfolio, and the bank's fee for this service is based upon the market value of the portfolio.

Some banks offer their investment service in conjunction with a high-interest account. This type of 'asset management' package is specifically aimed at customers with a largish sum (say £20,000 plus) in cash or marketable securities. The bank keeps track of these securities and brings them together in a monthly statement. The customer can then make decisions such as the buying or selling of stocks and shares, which the bank can in turn implement. Large surpluses on current account can be automatically transferred by the bank into a high-interest investment account. In addition, a typical package might include some kind of automatic borrowing facility and a cashpoint or credit card facility. Its 'all in oneness' is designed to attract otherwise busy customers who are happy to allow the bank to keep track of their money and investments for the basic price of a quarterly subscription fee.

UNIT TRUSTS

Some customers come to the bank with specific requests about putting their savings into a unit trust. Unit trusts are a form of investment designed for the small saver who wants to benefit from the capital growth of shareholdings without the risks associated with buying shares in specific companies. Frequently, unit trust companies are subsidiaries of the banks. The banks themselves may be either the manager of the fund or are often the trustees of the fund, who ensure scrupulous dealings with investors' money. At one time, for example, Barclays Bank managed the Unicorn group of trusts (purchased by Martins Bank in 1967). Management of a unit trust fund involves buying the portfolio of securities on behalf of unit holders and managing the portfolio in a way which meets the funds objectives of capital appreciation or a regular income and a spread of risk.

The supervisory role of the trustee bank means that the bank has to ensure that the managers of the unit trust fund keep within the parameters laid down in the trust deed and the regulations issued by the Department of Trade. All the guidelines are designed to protect the interests of the unit holders. This type of overseeing role is a logical extension of the banks' trusteeship in other areas.

The saver who opts to put funds into a unit trust can be well advised by the clearing banks, who with their branch networks are in a strong position to market their particular unit trusts on a country-wide basis. The saver can use a savings plan whereby an agreed monthly amount is contributed to the unit trust of the saver's choice. There is a huge variety of unit trusts to choose from and they do of course represent competition for the banks for the holding of customer's money. This aspect of unit trusts is more fully developed in Chapter 12.

If a customer wishes to simply 'save' a lump sum, or to build up a lump sum by regular deposits, banks do cater for this need. All the clearing banks offer a cheque account for investors which combines a high return on money with easy access to funds. There may be a minimum level of investment required in return for a competitive interest rate. A special cheque book is issued with a cheque guarantee card so that the deposits may be used when required. The use of cash cards and lobby services further enhance availability.

Insurance services

Another major service offered by the banks, particularly the clearing banks, is acting as insurance brokers. The banks act as intermediaries, for example, in placing investment funds in various forms of insurance contracts. As with many of the newer services, the bank will either have a department whose sole function is to develop and run the service, or the bank concerned may prefer to set up a subsidiary company. Again the branch banking network and the personal contact that the managers and staff have with customers concerning their financial affairs, puts the bank in an enviable position to introduce the notion of insurance to a customer and to offer to make all the arrangements.

The thrust of the service offered by the banks and their offshoot companies is that of meeting the changing financial needs of the customer. These needs range over a lifetime – from house purchase to providing for children's education to planning for retirement, for example.

Many of these financial needs can be met by arranging for life assurance cover which makes a lump-sum payment on the death of the assured and/or gives an endowment sum on a particular date, whichever is the sooner. Thus life assurance policies act as a vehicle for saving and investment as well as providing cover for, say, the death of the breadwinner in a family. Some assurance cover is linked to authorized unit trusts so that the value of the policy on maturity or surrender is based on the value of the underlying units. There is a great variety of life policies on offer, including mortgage protection assurance, children's assurance and personal pension schemes, to name but a few. The bank manager can ascertain the cover and savings needs of the customer and match those needs with an appropriate policy.

The banks can also point out to their customers the contingencies that they are exposed to, apart from death. Ownership of possessions carries the risk of theft and loss. Going away on holiday, particularly abroad, exposes the customer to certain risks such as illness and/or personal injury. Car driving is a dangerous business and an illegal one if appropriate insurance is not carried. The bigger banks claim to be willing to arrange insurance cover for all the main contingencies such as marine or fire insurance as well as some of the minor ones, such as insuring against bad weather or the birth of twins. The bank's insurance service might be particularly useful to those running their own business, either as sole traders, partnerships or companies. The entrepreneur has to provide his or her own pension, guard against burdensome tax liabilities and minimize business risks such as producing faulty and dangerous products. There may also be compulsory insurance requirements. If staff are employed, for example, the law requires that the employer takes out an employer's liability insurance policy. As with any insurance broking service, there is a commission taken by the broking agency and the customer pays for the premiums on the policy itself.

Loans

As we saw in Chapter 7, individuals who want a large sum for the purchase of a specific good – a car or a washing machine, for example – may be offered loans by a bank. Loans enable the customer to purchase the item immediately (and perhaps when the need is greatest) rather than deferring purchase until the purchase price had been accumulated by saving.

Hire purchase

An extention of this traditional role of lending has been for banks to enter the field of hire purchase. The clearing banks own subsidiaries and have interests in finance companies which deal in hire purchase. Under a hire purchase agreement (or a consumer credit agreement as it is now more frequently known), the customer gets possession of goods which belong to the finance house or bank. The customer then pays for these goods by weekly or monthly instalments. At the end of the instalment period, ownership or title to the goods is transferred to the hirer/customer.

Instalment finance can be used by a business or individual to buy capital goods. Businesses also have the option of leasing, which is fully examined later in this chapter.

CASH-MANAGEMENT SERVICES

The corporate customer may be interested in the cash-management service offered by the banks. This service provides company treasurers with details of their bank balances on world-wide accounts. The inter-company position can be read off from one computer statement from a single source and if necessary in a single currency.

The supply of information is not hampered by the fact that transactions are completed in local and diverse currencies. The corporate subscriber is linked into the world-wide time-sharing network of Automatic Data Processing Network Services. The subscriber can request selected information – from balances only on each account, to full details of all transactions passing through the account. For a multinational company, control over its cash flow and liquid assets is greatly enhanced by this facility.

Increasingly, banks have attempted to market their services by first identifying a client group with specific needs. Existing services are then gathered together and developed with the identified customer in mind. In recent years the banks have recognized the needs of the business sector – particularly small businesses – for financial information and advice. Large companies had in-house resources or could turn to the merchant banks, whose business relationship with corporate customers often started with advice on public quotations on the Stock Exchange. Small businesses – whether firms or companies – tended to have limited contact with the bank beyond the occasional overdraft arrangement and were often unaware of the range of services that they could benefit from. The clearing banks have responded to the challenge of meeting this market by offering business advisory services.

Business advisory services

The format of the scheme varies from bank to bank, but the main tenet, common to all, is that specially trained business consultants work with the small firm for a short period. During this time the business consultant concentrates on the financial management of the firm. This might mean an assessment of aspects of the business such as management targets, budget performance, the costing system, pricing policy, credit-control procedures, cash flow, stock control, accounting procedures and the management information systems. The consultant looks for ways to improve these aspects so that the customer makes better use of capital, is better informed about the business and the business is run more efficiently. Frequently, the bank will make no charge for this service, but the bank stands to benefit in the long term. At the very least, the lending risk to that firm is reduced, and at best the increasing prosperity of the customer is bound to benefit the banker. The professional approach offered by the bank reassures small businesses that their particular problems are understood. In addition, the detailed study of the firm may provide the bank with an opportunity to promote other services of interest to business such as leasing, insurance cover or personal pension schemes.

Computer services

Some banks offer computer services, providing the customer time on one of its own computers. The customer cannot justify the full-time use of a computer, but may from time to time benefit from access to one. Various packages exist to help the small business person on all aspects of the business. The stock control, management information and payroll functions are all facilitated by the use of a computer rather than a manual system. Indeed, some banks offer a pay service designed to take over the time-consuming job of payroll from the entrepreneur. Included in the service is the crediting of pay direct to employees' bank accounts, or the issuing of wage and salary cheques. If the business prefers to pay its workforce in cash, cash analyses can be supplied.

The pay service can handle all deductions from employees' income tax, national insurance and pension contributions. Changes in employee legislation can be automatically taken care of. Appropriate end-of-year tax documentation can also be produced.

Leasing

A leasing arrangement is one in which the business customer agrees to rent a capital asset owned by someone else. By capital asset we mean large items of plant and machinery essential to the production of the businesses' goods and services. For a farm, for example, leased plant and equipment may be grain storage-facilities or tractors and ploughing machinery. The plant and equipment technically belongs to the lessor, although possession and use remains in the hands of the lessee. In this respect it differs from hire purchase schemes (mentioned earlier in this chapter), in which the contract specifies that the hirer acquires the goods at the end of the hire purchase period.

The banks offer this sort of service through subsidiary and associated companies. The company who owns the equipment makes a charge for its use. The person borrowing the equipment has only to pay a weekly/monthly charge, rather than make a large outlay all at once. Leasing, then, can be of mutual satisfaction to both parties in the bargain. The banks do not have to rely on an existing banker–customer relationship for their leasing business. A leasing agreement can be struck with a customer or non-customer alike, each bank and finance house bidding for the business on a competitive basis.

Factoring

The business of factoring can be described as that of the management, and sometimes the purchase of business debts. The major clearing banks became involved in the 1960s, either through subsidiaries or associated companies.

In general, the factoring services consist of four main functions:

1. The bank manages the trade debts of the business customer (this means keeping the sales accounts ledgers and sending out the invoices).
2. The bank can also offer to do 'credit control', that is to tell the business customer who to offer credit to, and on what terms.
3. The bank may offer the business customer protection if one of the trade debtors fails to pay. The bank carries the risk of any bad debts.
4. The bank could collect the payments from the trade debtors on behalf of its business customer as they fall due.

The business customer, then, is relieved of the responsibility of running a sales ledger. They would normally pay a percentage (based on the business's annual sales) for the service, the size of the percentage depending on factors such as the degree of difficulty and the risks of, say, bad debts.

Like other banking services, the factoring service can be tailored to the needs of the customer. It is possible, for example, for the customer to be fixed with final responsibility for debts, whilst enjoying all other aspects of the factoring service. This version of the factoring service is known as recourse factoring (as opposed to non-recourse factoring), because the factor has full recourse to the customer in the event of a debtor's failure to pay up.

For the exporter, the export factoring service can do much to alleviate the risks and uncertainties of selling abroad. Export factoring does the same job for the exporting business as domestic factoring does for domestic firms and companies.

The factor takes on the burden of chasing slow payers in other countries and the unpredictability of an exchange rate that can move adversely between the date of the invoice and the date of payment. International banks and their subsidiaries can arrange for collection of money through their overseas network. The bank can account to the customer in either the currency of the invoice or in the sterling equivalent.

Trustee and executor services

The term 'trustee services' can embrace a variety of work. We have already discussed the trustee role in relation to unit trusts, for example. We can start here with estate management – or executor and trustee business, as it is more commonly known.

The business is the responsibility of special trustee branches or subsidiaries of the banks. Executorship consists of administering a deceased person's *estate* – the word meaning the possessions and money owned by the dead person at the time of death. The job of administering these possessions involves gathering the assets together, paying off outstanding debts and expenses, including any tax liability on the estate, and ensuring that the estate is distributed according to the will of the deceased. The executor is accountable for these actions to the persons named in the will, who will inherit the dead person's possessions.

The bank becomes an executor by being so named in the will of the deceased. Branch managers are often consulted by customers prior to the making of a will about their financial concerns, such as how to provide for dependants. The customer can appoint anyone of full age and sound mind to administer their estate after death. The customer may opt for a relative or friend, for example, or perhaps for the services of a professional person such as a solicitor.

The cost to the customer of using the bank's executor service is covered by the terms of the will. The document contains a clause entitling the bank to deduct its fees from the value of the estate. Banks' charging systems vary, but the most commonly used is that of a percentage of the value of the estate. In addition, there may be a setting up fee, an annual fee for administration and a vacating fee on termination. Percentage charges by themselves cannot really reflect accurately the time spent on an estate – some being very much more complex than others.

Not every bank customer or individual makes a will. If a person dies intestate – that is without making a will – the distribution of assets has to be undertaken in accordance with the provisions of the Family Law (Inheritance) Act 1969. The bank may still be appointed to carry out the distribution, although technically in this situation the bank is known as an administrator. The bank can also be brought in if the person named as executor in the will has died or is no longer willing to act in this capacity. It is also possible that the bank acts as joint executor with an individual, if so appointed by the deceased in his or her will.

Income tax service

There are tax savings to be enjoyed for the self-employed person who saves via a pension scheme. The banks may bring this fact to the attention of the customer who uses the income tax mangement service of the bank. The service is designed to relieve the customer of the paperwork associated with income tax returns. It also can offer expertise which will ensure that the customer claims all the pertinent allowances and pays no more tax than is necessary. The tax departments are in a position to suggest means of minimizing tax liability such as establishing a trust or contributing to a pension scheme.

Home banking service

The services offered by banks to customers will continue to develop and change as the needs of the customer change. As well as market-led changes, developments in technology will reshape the type of services on offer and their delivery. One development, initiated by the Bank of Scotland, is that of the home (and office) banking service. This service enables individuals to monitor their accounts, order statements and cheque books, pay bills and transfer funds between accounts, from their living rooms. It is all made possible by either using a television and telephone which links up Prestel with a bank computer. Alternatively, the customer can use their own home or business computer together with a modem. The convenience of managing one's own money from the home is an obvious attraction of home banking, as is the freedom to deal with financial affairs outside traditional banking hours. For the user who also has a cash card, almost all banking needs can be met at the initiative of the customer and without the need to enter a branch bank.

The individual who wishes to subscribe to the service can call up on the television screen full details of all the accounts held by the customer at the bank. This is, in addition to the regular printed statement, sent to the customer. Bills can be paid by the customer filling in a bill-payment mandate which gives details of the creditor account. The variable details, such as the actual amount to be transmitted and the date of the transmission are keyed in, as and when a bill is received. The service allows for instructions to be pending for up to thirty days. This enables the customer to benefit from any free period of credit without the worry of remembering when the bill finally falls due.

Money can readily be transferred between the customer's own accounts, and the customer can, by switching, gain maximum advantage of prevailing interest rates. Users may opt to open an investment account for this very reason. Variations in the rates will be published from time to time, perhaps via a teletext service such as Prestel.

For businesses, the need for an accurate and up-to-date picture of the organization's financial standing is crucial. The Bank of Scotland's home banking service offers a cash management facility which identifies the cleared funds within each account. Other banks offer similar services to corporate customers and may adopt and promote home banking with this feature in mind. For businesses there is, as for individuals, a saving of time in not having to visit bank branches. Financial management can continue at weekends and in the evenings, irrespective of bank opening hours. Both the individual and corporate customer are given codes and passwords to obtain access to their accounts. The password is chosen by the customer and can be varied at any time. The system can have additional safeguards built in, such as an automatic close-down of operations if there are several attempts at access using the wrong code. This is designed to catch any unauthorized person who attempts to 'break-in' to the system by making random guesses as to what the code may be.

The cost to the customer of this service (apart from the initial cost of purchasing a television or computer and installing a telephone) is that of a monthly subscription fee. The size of the fee is linked to the number of users or 'keycard' holders, and to whether it is an individual or business customer. Transaction charges are largely free, and worked out on a similar basis to current-account charges. The user may also have to meet Prestel and telephone charges, levied by British Telecom.

Both here and in the USA, home banking is as yet a relatively small segment of the market, but banks here foresee that there could well be a demand for home banking in the future. At least two major clearing banks are known to have tested systems that they have developed; the building societies are also interested. In the next decade, then, the focus of services may switch slightly away from what services are required, to how those services may be delivered – what is most convenient for the customer. Then we may see an expansion of home banking that could change the face of our high streets.

Conclusion

Throughout this chapter we have attempted to list the services offered by the banks. What the service consists of, what it costs and who might benefit from using the service.

Identifying an actual or potential user of a service is something the marketing departments of banks have been working on over the last few years. The general thrust of marketing strategy has been to emphasize that banks can provide a comprehensive 'cradle to grave' service that meets all the banking and financial needs of a customer. From the banks' point of view the earlier the customer begins the banking relationship the better. There is some evidence to suggest that once a customer opens an account, that same customer is reluctant to switch to a competitor. All the banks then have been keen to attract a junior and young market and offer special inducements such as a record voucher or book token to the youngster. Having 'caught' a new customer, the banks reckon to be able to meet his or her financial needs throughout that customer's life – and beyond, if executor work is involved!

To make the general public more aware of the services banks offer (particularly the 15.5 million adults who do not have a bank account), the services are increasingly being offered as 'packages' to particular client groups. The package attempts to bring together all the services that are thought relevant for that group. For example, all major banks have targeted students as being a desirable client group. Every year some 60,000 students begin full-time university and polytechnic courses. As students they are unlikely to be already banking with a competitor. In addition, they are likely to be the future high earners in the country, since better-qualified individuals tend to attract higher salaries, and if the banking relationship goes smoothly in these college years, the banks may have earned themselves a life-long customer. Some banks, in their efforts to win student accounts, have located branches near to the potential customers – on campus sites, close to halls of residence, in university towns, and so on. The National Westminster Bank has been the most successful in this strategy: some 300 of its branches are positioned in or near to campuses. Other banks rely more heavily on advertising in the national and local press, particularly at the start of the academic year. All banks now offer a student package of free banking whilst the account is in credit, and a limited overdraft facility. The charges for overdrawn accounts vary slightly. Beyond these two basics (often with cash cards thrown in as well), the banks offer a variety of 'freebies' – a free wallet, an alarm clock, a coach card which enables the holder to buy cheap fares on the National Express and a directory of summer jobs, are a sample of the current crop of inducements. Some packages include loans at special interest rates on graduation or for parents having to subsidize local authority grants. All offer advice on how to minimize the tax liability parents attract, for example by recommending the use of a deed of covenant.

The student package is only one of the dozen or so packages geared to a specific group of customers. They range from a 'starting work' package (designed to follow on from the junior savings clubs) to packages aimed at home buyers (mortgages), home occupiers (home contents insurance) and pensioners (financial strategies on retirement and wills and trusts). Where the service does not neatly identify with a particular age group or life stage, a broad heading is used with the minor services collected beneath it. Thus a 'travel services' leaflet can remind the reader not only of the different methods of payment available in foreign currencies but also insurance cover for individuals and motorists and general advice on travelling abroad.

As the financial services sector continues to increase its competitive thrust, we can anticipate also that marketing strategy will keep in mind how the services are delivered, as much as what is delivered. The user will be the reference point as banks become more sensitive to market demand. The customer must therefore benefit.

Domestic services of banks

Self-examination questions

1 What is the relationship between banker and customer when the customer deposits an envelope with the bank for safe-keeping?
2 Describe the facility available to a local retailer that will enable him to deposit his funds in a bank after the bank has closed.
3 Describe the procedure you as a banker would adopt when a customer telephones you with a request to purchase shares in a well-known public limited company.
4 What is a unit trust?
5 Name some of the insurance services available from a bank.
6 What do you understand by a 'business advisory service'?
7 What is leasing?
8 How does factoring assist a businessman to overcome his cash liquidity problems?
9 State the difference between a trustee and an executor.
10 What do you understand by 'home banking'?

9 Foreign services of banks

This extends the bank's traditional spheres of services into attempting to meet the needs of the individual traveller, going abroad, whether a customer or not. In addition, corporate customers will require the foreign services that banks can offer in order to carry out their dealings with parties based in other countries.

Foreign currency

Given the very large increase in the number of holidaymakers travelling abroad, the banks have been happy to provide foreign currency for those trips.

The branches, particularly small ones, will not necessarily retain stocks of all the currencies requested, but will be able to meet orders for currency within a period of about one week. The sort of currency dealing is confined mainly to notes, although on rare occasions only coins are obtainable. Since coins are bulky and heavy and thus more expensive to deal with, banks will purchase these from a customer only as a special favour, but will not consider a coin of small denomination.

The bank sells the foreign currency to the customer at a stated exchange rate, for example £1 might be exchanged for, say £1.35. The exchange rate changes daily and the selling price for the currency will be pitched at a lower rate than the buying price, since the bank needs to make a profit for the currency service. Additionally, it will make a commission charge.

As well as providing the currency, the banks can advise customers on any foreign-exchange regulations that affect the importation and exportation of the currency of the country concerned. Some countries, for example, particularly in the Eastern bloc, do not allow foreign visitors to purchase their currency before embarking on their journey, nor return home with any local currency. No doubt this must be an inducement to visitors to spend all the local money they have before leaving, or to pay in Western currencies, which are in short supply.

In the past the UK herself has had exchange control regulations which prohibited travellers abroad from taking sterling (or its foreign currency equivalent) above a prescribed limit out of the country. Currently, no such exchange control exists. Banks will often buy back any surplus currency from the returning traveller at the current rate of exchange.

Since the advent of 'bureau-de-change' facilities, banks have been competing for the foreign-exchange business. Bureaux-de-change are open for very long hours and sited in popular tourist areas. Also, many hotels and stores offer a bureau-de-change facility for their clients. The banks' response has been to lengthen their opening hours and in some cases to set up its own network of bureaux, as Lloyds did via its Lewis's bank subsidiary, which set up bureaux de change in some of Lewis's stores.

Traveller's cheques

The holidaymaker or business traveller abroad can order cheques in either foreign currency or sterling. These cheques are for fixed amounts and in sterling usually £5, £10, £20, £50 and £100, known as traveller's cheques. They enable the user to buy goods and services abroad without the risk of carrying loose cash or banknotes.

On issue, the bank cashier will insist that the purchaser signs his or her name on each traveller's cheque. When the person is abroad and a shop, hotel or restaurant is offered a traveller's cheque in payment, it must be countersigned in the presence of the paying agent, who will check that the holder's signature matches that already on the traveller's cheque. This is a safeguard against theft.

Should any traveller's cheque be stolen, then the true owner should contact the issuing bank or, if this is not praticable, the issuing bank's correspondent or branch in the foreign country. A list of all overseas correspondents is given to all purchasers of traveller's cheques. The number(s) of the stolen cheque(s) should be given and the total amount is reimbursed immediately, providing an indemnity has been signed and that evidence has been produced that the loss has been reported to the local police.

Traveller's cheques have no maturity date and can, if necessary, be kept from one overseas visit to another – although this would be impractical for the once-a-year holidaymaker. On issue, a commission is paid to the issuing bank and when encashed abroad, if the cheque is in sterling, a collection charge is made. In some countries a stamp duty is also payable. The majority of UK travellers usually take sterling travellers cheques, but many will take traveller's cheques in foreign currency. For example, those visiting the USA are advised to take US dollar traveller's cheques. Traveller's cheques are also available in all major international currencies – Swiss francs, German marks, Yen, and so on. When encashing a currency cheque in the country of origin a collection charge is not usually made, and as the amount is in local currency, no exchange commission is payable.

Passports

For the traveller who needs to renew or obtain a passport, a visit to the bank for travellers cheques can be combined with a submission of the passport form. Using the bank's passport service, the application form is countersigned by the bank manager, who also verifies the likeness of the photographs (two must be attached to each passport application form), and send the form to the passport office. The intending traveller can collect the passport from the bank together with his foreign currency. A charge is usually made for this service.

Eurocheque scheme

Under this scheme the customer is given a special cheque book and a cheque guarantee card. With the latter, payment is guaranteed to any overseas bank within the Eurocheque scheme that cashes a cheque for the customer. The banks within the scheme will usually display the EC symbol. The cheque is drawn in local currency, so that at the time of receiving funds no exchange commission is paid. On receipt of the cheque in London, it is converted into sterling and the customer is debited with the amount drawn, plus the paying banker's commission.

At the moment the holder of the cheque book and card is permitted to draw two cheques per day, up to the equivalent of £50 each.

Foreign exchange

Corporate customers, or other forms of business organizations, may also require foreign currency to finance business deals with foreign parties. The difficulties these importers and exporters face is that exchange rates may fluctuate significantly – the pound may rise or fall against the dollar by more than 10 per cent, say, in the space of a week or so. It is possible that the direction of the movement will benefit the home-based trader. Exporters of Scottish goods to the USA, for example, were pleased to see recently a downward lurch in the value of the sterling against dollar; the 'bottom' was $1.05 to the pound. This made the Scottish goods cheaper on the American market and the volume of sales was therefore greater. There is a risk, of course, that the movement in the exchange rate could equally go against the interests of the UK trader and so wipe out all or most of his profits.

To eliminate the risks associated with moving exchange rates, the business person can arrange with the bank for a contract known as a 'fixed forward exchange contract'. This contract is legally binding on all parties. Under this fixed forward contract, a particular day in the future is specified for the purchase or sale of a given amount of currency. That way the business person can be assured of a calculated profit. For example, an importer will know that on a given date he will have to purchase a specific amount of foreign currency to pay for his imports at a given rate of exchange. He will therefore know exactly, in sterling terms, how much the goods will cost him; he can then calculate his selling price and thus calculate his profit. Similarly, an exporter will sell foreign currency at a fixed rate at a given date in the future, so that no matter which way the exchange rate moves, he is assured of a known profit.

Bills of exchange

Another means of settling debts abroad would be by using a bill of exchange. Like a cheque, a bill of exchange is a type of negotiable instrument; unlike cheques, however, they may not necessarily be drawn on a banker.

In law, a bill of exchange has been defined as:

> an unconditional order, in writing, addressed by one person to another, signed by the person giving it, requiring the person to whom it is addressed, to pay on demand or at a fixed or determinable future time a sum certain in money to, or to the order of, a specified person or to bearer. (Bills of Exchange Act 1882, section 3)

Like a cheque, a bill can be used to pay for goods or services rendered from one party to another. At its simplest the bill is a written instruction from the drawer (the creditor) direct to the drawee (the debtor) to settle the debt by making a payment to a specified person or bearer.

This acknowledgement of indebtedness might specify an immediate settlement, or settlement at a future date. The drawee's bank would arrange for payment to be made to the drawer's bank on the appropriate date. Both banks would charge a commission for their services. Frequently, a bill of exchange is used to pay off a debt that the drawer owes to a third party. So the drawer directs that payment be made to someone other than himself. As in a two-party bill, the bill is accepted by the drawee for eventual settlement. The payee's bank will present the bill for payment on the due date, and the banks involved collect commission for the transaction.

The use of the bill of exchange as a means of settling debts between parties based in foreign countries offers several advantages for the business customer. A bill can be drawn up with a time for payment set at some future date. So an overseas buyer has a period of credit after acceptance during which he or she can sell the goods and raise the funds to settle the debts at maturity. Or the bill as a negotiable instrument can easily be negotiated on to settle some other indebtedness. Or, the bank or some other financial institution can discount the bill before maturity, so that they can provide the payee or holder with funds for much-needed working capital. A bill can be drawn up in sterling or in foreign currency. For the exporter or importer the use of a bill of exchange is important when such an instrument is used for the collection of payment relevant to goods shipped, and the parties agree that ownership will not pass from one to the other until payment or acceptance of the bill of exchange has been made.

Documentary collections

Where there is very little trust between parties, and the exporter does not want to lose ownership before he has been notified that payment has been made or his bill has been accepted, he may agree with the importer to draw a bill on him and present the documents, with the bill attached, for payment via his bank. The procedure is as follows:

1 UK exporter hands shipping documents (e.g. invoice, bills of lading, etc.), with bill of exchange attached, to his bank.
2 At the same time the UK exporter instructs his or her bank to deliver documents against payment (D/P) or deliver documents against acceptance (D/A).
3 Bank will send documents with bill of exchange to their correspondent or branch to importer's country, specifying the instructions.
4 The collecting bank will contact the importer and request either payment or acceptance of the bill and then hand over the documents as authorized.
5 Importer who wishes to obtain goods will either accept the bill or pay the bill, collect the documents, obtain the goods.
6 With a D/A collection, the collecting bank will advise the remitting bank that the bill and the date of maturity have been accepted. At maturity, they will re-present the bill for payment and on payment advise the remitting bank and remit the funds in accordance with instructions given.

There is an international agreement on documentary collections that is covered in a booklet issued by the International Chamber of Commerce called *Uniform Rules for Collection*.

Documentary credits

This is yet another service aimed at facilitating trade between parties. The service arises out of the need to reassure the exporter that payment will be made for the goods whilst assuring the importer that payment will not be made unless the documents presented are in accordance with his authority. In other words, an importer does not want to pay until he can get the goods he ordered and an exporter does not want to release the goods until he has been paid. There is no trust between the parties. To overcome this lack of trust, banks step into the shoes of both importer and exporter. How does this work?

1 Both parties agree to open a documentary credit.
2 The importer will instruct his bank to open a credit in favour of the exporter. The credit can either be revocable or irrevocable. This will be elaborated upon later, but the most usual is the irrevocable.
3 When opening the credit, the importer will state:
   - the amount of the credit
   - in whose favour the credit should be
   - date of expiry of the credit
   - whether it is to be revocable or irrevocable
   - advice by airmail or cable
   - description of the goods
   - documents required
   - whether partial shipment is permitted
   - whether transshipment is permitted
   - port of loading and port of discharge and name of vessel, if known.

An irrevocable documentary credit means that neither party can change the terms of the agreement without consent of the other. A revocable credit can have any or all of its terms amended by the importer, which puts the exporter in a weak position.

The bank that pays or negotiates the documents under the letter of credit, must ensure that the documents presented conform strictly to the terms and conditions of the credit. If they do not, then the bank must not pay without first obtaining the authority of the opener (importer). However, if the documents conform in every way to the credit, the paying banker must pay, as the credit states, 'we will honour your drafts on us'. This could apply even if, between the time of opening the credit and its eventual payment, the importer goes into liquidation. Should this happen, the bank – having no collateral – will retain the goods and sell them to obtain refund of the amount due.

In some instances the exporter does not know the standing of the issuing bank, so that he will request his own banker or the advising bank to add its own confirmation to the credit. This confirmed credit means that there is an additional undertaking that a bank, known in the exporter's country, has confirmed that it will make the necessary payment.

By using a documentary credit, both the exporter and importer are assured that payment will be made and received by the appropriate parties.

Economic and trade information

These bulletins are issued on a regular basis by banks. They contain information of interest to those engaged in foreign trade, including details of companies abroad who are looking to UK companies to supply particular goods. The banks can also service organizations that trade abroad in that they can frequently match up potential buyers and sellers. The bank can then advise on possible trading partners and can arrange for the credit status of the potential party to be determined, via its correspondent or branch.

Economic intelligence reports

Exporters are also supported by the information they can obtain from the economic intelligence departments of banks. It is the job of these departments to compile regular fact sheets concerning specific countries. These reports concern themselves with data on the economic and political profile of a country, together with trading information such as trade agreements, quotas, import regulations, and so on. Firms dealing in international trade can use this information to determine such matters as the price the product will sell for and the size of the market in the country concerned.

Bonds

When an overseas buyer of a major capital project – say, a large office block, ship, bridge or hospital – has entered into negotiations, he will require some assurance from the firm abroad that the work will be done in accordance with the contract and in the agreed time. To assure the overseas buyer, the UK company will, on tendering for the contract, request his bank to issue a tender bond, which is basically a guarantee that if the contract was offered to him, then he would be prepared to complete the contract as stipulated. Without being penalized, he could not, after being offered the contract suddenly, change his mind and refuse to accept.

On acceptance of the contract, the buyer will request the contractor to have available to him a performance bond, which again is issued by a UK bank so that if there was any fault in the completion of the task, the buyer could claim the amount stipulated in the performance bond.

Banks will issue performance bonds providing they regard their customer as being in a position to carry through the performance. In any event, the bank issuing a performance bond would normally require an indemnity, occasionally with some collateral, from its customer against a possible call.

The method of issue is as follows: the UK bank, at the request of the customer, will issue a bond in favour of buyer's bank abroad; on receipt of this bond, the buyer's bank will issue its bond in favour of the buyer.

Foreign services of banks

Self-examination questions

1 Describe a traveller's cheque.
2 Describe the Eurocheque system.
3 What do you understand by a fixed forward foreign exchange contract?
4 Define a bill of exchange.
5 How does a D/A collection differ from a D/P collection?
6 Name the set of instructions that govern the collection of financial and commercial documents.
7 Name at least four points that you are likely to see on a documentary credit.
8 Distinguish between an irrevocable and a revocable documentary credit.
9 Before a trader enters into international trade, what reports and information can be given to him by a bank?
10 When a major capital project is in the course of being negotiated, state two bonds that could be given to a buyer, to assure him that the contract will be completed within the terms stated.

10 Transfer of funds: the clearing system

Every single working day all banks receive cheques payable to their customers either across the counter or by post for the credit of their various accounts. The banks as agents for collection have the duty of presenting all of these cheques for payment and having credited the customer's account, then receiving reimbursement themselves.

History of the clearing system

The clearing system began over 200 years ago, when the clerks of the various banks in London used to take the cheques paid in by their customers, sort them into bank order then walk round each bank, presenting these cheques for payment and taking back to their own bank sums of money given in settlement. Like any other commercial activity, the business of banking increased, not only with the number of cheques in circulation but also the number of banks that opened in the City of London and the West End. The clerks, who knew each other, thus decided to short-circuit the system and unofficially agreed to meet at some convenient place – as history tells us, a coffee house – to exchange the cheques drawn on their own banks: any differences in the amounts due could then quickly and easily be settled.

The employers, who eventually learnt of the system, realized that there were advantages not only to their employees but to themselves as well. Of course, it saved hours of labour, walking the streets of London. In addition, under the new system it was no longer necessary for the banks – which in those days only had one office, perhaps two – to keep large sums of money to meet the presentation of cheques. The surplus cash could be used to invest and increase profits.

The banks, anxious to improve the system, hired a room

for the purpose of exchanging cheques. The system expanded and in 1833, in 10 Lombard Street, the first clearing house was established.

This system continued, but until 1854 the membership of the clearing house was restricted to the private banks only. At that date the joint-stock banks were allowed to have a seat on the Committee of London Clearing banks. These clearing banks expanded their sphere of operations, so that all towns and cities in the UK had a representative of at least three or four clearing banks. The major cities, of course, had quite a number of branches of all clearing banks.

Until the middle of this century there were the following members of the Clearing House:

Bank of England
Barclays Bank
Coutts & Co.
District Bank
Glyn Mills
Lloyds Bank
Martins Bank
Midland Bank
National Bank
National Provincial Bank
Westminster Bank
Williams & Deacons Bank

Added to these were the various banks that were part of the 'walks' system. They consisted of the Scottish and Irish banks, the few foreign banks, merchant banks, and so on. The cheques for each bank were in fact taken by messenger to each bank, who then gave the messenger a banker's payment, in settlement of the total of the cheques presented. The walks system still exists today.

Credits that were paid into a branch for a customer of another branch, or for the credit of a branch of another bank, were actually sent by post. You can imagine the situation. At the end of the day, a clerk sat down and wrote out claim forms for each and every credit, placed them together, wrote out an envelope, then sent them individually to the banks or branches concerned. At times the volume of work was quite substantial, particularly at the end of the month, on quarterly days, and so on. There were no automated ways of dealing with these items, nor was there then a credit clearing system.

The present organization

It is only as recently as 1 December 1985 that the organizations responsible for the clearing services in England, Scotland and Wales were reorganized to oversee all the various forms of clearing.

The former major organizations, the Committee of London Clearing Banks and the Scottish Bankers Association, were dissolved and the Committee of London and Scottish Bankers (CLSB) was formed as a constituent of the British Bankers Association. The CLSB concerns itself in dealing with a wide range of issues on behalf of its members, including regulatory, legislative and fiscal matters.

Coinciding with the establishment of the CLSB, the Association of Payment Clearing Services (APACS) became operational and is the body responsible for the clearing systems, which are legally three independent limited companies. They are:

Cheque & Credit Clearing Co. Ltd
CHAPS & Town Clearing Co. Ltd
Bankers Automated Clearing Services Ltd

Eventually, a fourth clearing company, EFT-POS – Electronic Funds Transfer Point of Sale – will be set up.

With the mergers and amalgamations of various banks in the 1960s, a majority of names have disappeared from the original list of clearing banks. Overall there are now fourteen banks who are represented on at least one clearing company. Many of the original names have disappeared and others have taken their place.

Cheque & Credit Clearing Co. Ltd

The members of this clearing company are as follows: Bank of England, Barclays Bank, Central Trustee Savings Bank, Co-operative Bank, Lloyds Bank, Midland Bank, National Girobank, National Westminster Bank and Royal Bank of Scotland. The purpose of this clearing company is to deal with the vast majority of cheques and credits presented over the counter at the various banks and their branches.

CLEARING PROCEDURES

In order to explain the workings of this company it is worth looking at the procedure from the collecting bank to the paying bank. Assume that on a Monday morning Mr England pays in a credit into his bank – Barclays Bank, Kings Cross. This credit contains a cheque for £50 drawn by Mr Scotland on his account at the Royal Bank of Scotland, Sheffield. Once the credit and cheques/cash have been agreed and the amount filled is completed, the cheques are listed and sorted. Mr Scotland's cheque, with others, is sorted into the Royal Bank of Scotland batch, listed again, and with all other cheques and their appropriate lists, together with a summary, are sent either by post or security van to the clearing department of Barclays Bank. With current computer methods, some branches of banks do not sort the cheques paid in, but make one complete list, then leave it to the computer sorter in the clearing department to do this sorting. On the Tuesday morning the clearing department of Barclays Bank will receive the bundle of cheques from this branch, and indeed every branch of the bank, proceed to extract the bundles of cheques for each bank in the clearing system, plus the bundles for the miscellaneous banks. The bundles of cheques for the Royal Bank of Scotland are given to representatives of that bank, while the Royal Bank of Scotland will in return give to their representatives all the cheques they have on Barclays Bank. The exchange of cheques, as you will see from the statistics in Tables 2 and 3, is quite formidable. The difference between the totals is settled by a draft on the Bank of England, who is of course the bankers' bank and through whom all clearing and inter-bank indebtedness is settled.

The clearing department then proceeds, with the use of its computers, to sort all the cheques received from other banks and from its own branches as well, into branch order. This

Table 2 Clearing statistics: volume (thousands of items)

Year	General debit clearing Inter-bank	General debit clearing Inter-branch	Town clearing Inter-bank	Town clearing Inter-branch	Credit clearing Inter-bank	Credit clearing Inter-branch
1972	784,583	342,747	3,601	817	116,526	133,487
1973	840,683	372,228	3,885	889	122,013	143,849
1974	880,292	389,918	4,053	910	127,732	153,687
1975	959,547	424,538	4,172	914	138,181	160,011
1976	1,043,556	423,607	4,381	899	159,357	170,570
1977	1,110,790	444,482	4,487	889	167,149	178,853
1978	1,212,161	460,046	4,457	846	180,105	184,838
1979	1,310,985	462,885	5,098	937	195,940	195,094
1980	1,453,702	493,625	4,969	945	213,869	208,104
1981	1,500,888	523,553	4,794	913	202,151	212,253
1982	1,559,997	545,874	4,848	907	180,823	233,529
1983[b]	1,672,404	552,193	5,072	929	177,935	249,769
1984	1,772,439	554,431	4,620	868	167,432	252,561
1985	1,861,649	587,793	4,473	814	164,790	251,358

Source: APACS Statistical Unit.
Notes: (a) Clearing House Automated Payment System commenced on 9 February 1984.
(b) Includes Girobank from 8 February 1983.

process may take as many as six sorts. At the end of the day, the clearing department has agreed its figures, then through the computer accountancy system, will debit the various customers with the amount of the cheque that they have drawn.

By the third day, Wednesday, the cheques have been presented to the drawee bank for final payment. All the customers accounts have been debited, the cheque provisionally paid, but the final payment must be made at the branch on whom it has been drawn. Should the branch wish to refuse payment for any reason, then it will do so. Assuming payment will be made, the clearing of a cheque

Automated Items					Total
BACS				CHAPS[a]	
Direct debits	Standing orders (inter-bank)	Other credits (inter-bank)	Standing orders (inter-branch)		
55,091	98,465	13,012	8,499	–	1,556,828
69,332	111,488	19,105	8,978	–	1,692,450
80,596	109,189	27,960	16,027	–	1,790,364
93,004	110,383	36,970	26,377	–	1,953,097
100,488	114,448	47,986	33,760	–	2,099,052
113,307	124,550	59,523	37,383	–	2,241,413
130,652	137,463	69,884	40,974	–	2,421,426
152,257	153,238	81,579	43.285	–	2,601,298
173,417	168,807	96,166	46,829	–	2,860,433
192,825	181,293	114,749	48,138	–	2,981,557
220,412	189,598	138,731	48,013	–	3,122,732
253,983	191,754	167,022	68,884	–	3,339,945
295,498	218,215	209,562	74,146	1,149	3,550,921
346,378	235,949	252,203	74,938	2,217	3,782,562

takes three working days. Figure 7 indicates how the system works.

Payment of a cheque presented through the clearing services

On receipt of the 'in clearing' in the morning, the recipient branch on whom the cheques are drawn, make the final decision whether to pay or not. One, perhaps two or even more persons are given the job of going through the cheques and ensuring that all is in order before payment is made. To signify that payment has been authorized, the person responsible will, normally in red ink, cancel the signature(s) of the drawer(s) usually by writing his own initials on top.

The following points should be checked:

1 *The cheque is drawn on the bank branch*: This may seem obvious, and is possibly overlooked, particularly as all cheques that are sorted by the computer are not usually

Table 3 Clearing statistics: value (£ million)[a]

Year	Paper Items				
	General debit clearing	Town clearing[b]		Credit clearing	
	Inter-bank	Inter-bank	Inter-branch	Inter-bank	Inter-branch
1972	123,749	947,372	186,918	14,006	54,273
1973	145,535	1,310,885	260,406	16,255	68,680
1974	160,952	1,479,238	290,437	18,580	78,062
1975	189,220	1,605,547	291,002	22,089	81,267
1976	223,361	1,980,730	321,251	26,946	98,667
1977	261,812	2,336,486	463,771	31,607	117,548
1978	301,647	2,544,254	521,119	36,887	135,204
1979	356,483	3,258,830	585,640	43,497	163,843
1980	405,690	4,051,203	782,172	51,853	193,400
1981	431,620	4,403,794	965,382	61,480	210,532
1982	479,424	5,291,926	1,172,284	62,563	239,395
1983[d]	543,267	6,257,551	1,337,195	67,978	264,030
1984	622,420	6,922,135	1,433,138	69,478	293,257
1985	680,207	7,463,677	1,730,196	72,616	331,461

Source: APACS Statistical Unit.

Notes: (a) No value figures are available for inter-branch general debit clearing or inter-branch standing orders.

(b) There were 107 city offices and branches in the Town Clearing at end 1985.

(c) Clearing House Automated Payment System commenced on 9 February 1984, but was originally restricted to payments of £10,000–£100,000; the upper limit was raised progressively and was finally removed on 1 May 1984.

(d) Includes Girobank from 8 February 1983.

despatched to the correct address; but there are still a number of cheques that are rejected by the reader/sorter and are manually sorted, so that it is possible, with human error, for a cheque to be sent to say, Margate instead of Moorgate.

As it happens, in the case of *Burnett* v. *National Westminster Bank* (1966) Burnett had an account at two branches of the

Automated Items			
BACS			CHAPS[c]

Direct debits	Standing orders (inter-bank)	Other credits (inter-branch)	
N/A	N/A	N/A	–
N/A	N/A	N/A	–
N/A	N/A	N/A	–
N/A	N/A	N/A	–
6,122	3,857	23,539	–
10,406	5,049	27,583	–
15,673	6,437	32,925	–
19,489	8,762	40,440	–
25,916	11,565	53,815	–
28,257	13,809	62,274	–
39,122	17,866	73,420	–
49,184	18,305	87,004	–
59,040	24,614	106,063	741,273
87,017	37,767	128,267	2,355,565

bank. He used a cheque drawn on one branch and changed the address at the top so that it was effectively drawn on the second branch. The following day he advised the second branch to stop the cheque, which they did. The computer, reading the magnetic characters, sent it to the first branch, which paid the cheque. Burnett sued the bank and he won his case.

Of course, it is possible to receive a cheque not drawn on the usual bank cheque form. It could be a blank cheque form issued by a club or a casino to one of its members for completion. He may then put in the correct bank; but if there are two branches in the same town or street, he could state the wrong address.

2 *Signature(s) agree with the mandate*: Under no circumstances can a bank debit a customer's account if the signature is

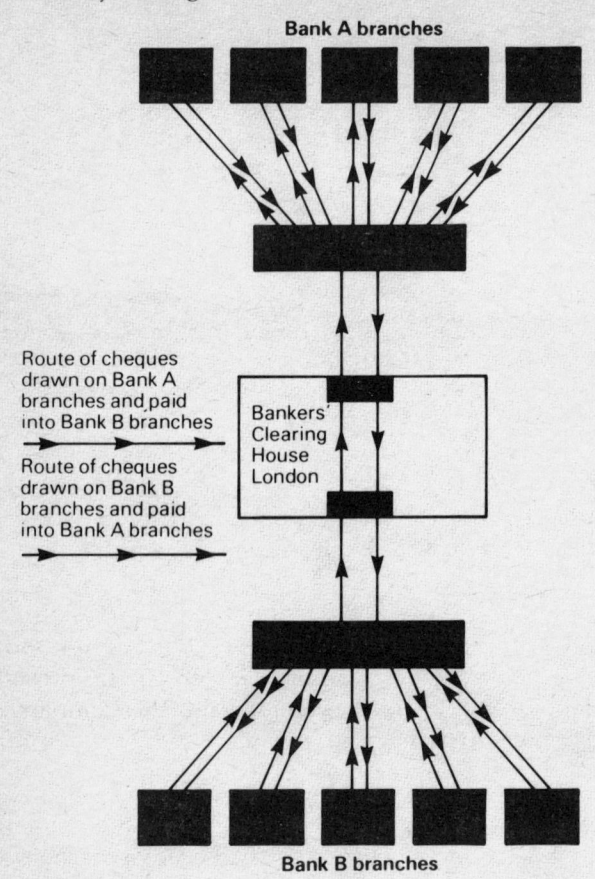

Figure 7 *The clearing system*
Source: Banking Education Service

Route of cheques drawn on Bank A branches and paid into Bank B branches

Route of cheques drawn on Bank B branches and paid into Bank A branches

forged or does not conform to the mandate held. Where the account is in a sole name, or where 'either to sign' on a joint account, there are few problems, but on large company accounts there may be a large number of signatories, of whom there may be two or perhaps three persons who can sign. Under these circumstances the bank should take care.

3 *Words and figures agree*: It is essential that the words and figures on the cheque agree. Should this *not* be the case, the

cheque should be returned. However, any difference in the amount may have been spotted by the collecting banks. If it has specified the amount that is being claimed (usually the lower amount), then the cheque is acceptable. On occasions, the amount may differ by a few pence only, in this case the lower amount is taken as being correct.

4 *The cheque has the correct date:* A cheque form which is post-dated is by definition not a cheque. It is not payable on demand, so that this cheque must not be paid. Should the bank do so, it is vulnerable to the possibility that the drawer may stop the cheque before the due date: also, the bank may have to return another cheque for lack of funds, because it paid a post-dated cheque. In both cases the bank has a problem. It is also within the realms of possibility that the drawer may die, go bankrupt or become mentally incapacitated. In all three cases, payment of a post-dated cheque will give the bank a problem.

By the same token, a cheque which is more than six months old is considered 'stale' and payment must be refused. This can happen when a shareholder forgets to present his dividend warrant; if it becomes stale, the company must either change the date with the usual signatures confirming the alteration, or a new warrant must be issued.

A cheque which has no date again must not be accepted, but returned unpaid.

In practical situations it is quite likely that just after 1 January many customers will write out a cheque and date it with the old year; banks should see whether the cheque number is in the current run of cheques and pay it in the normal way. Should the customer continue with this habit, he should be politely informed of his error.

5 *Payee*: A cheque must be paid to a specified person or to bearer. Thus a cheque where the payee's name has been omitted must be returned unpaid.

6 *Crossed two bankers*: Under the Bills of Exchange Act, if a cheque is crossed by two bankers, both clearing banks, then payment must be refused. This can happen; for example, a

person pays a cheque into his account through bank A, it is then returned unpaid due to a technicality, then presented again for payment through bank B. The paying bank must not pay this cheque unless an indemnity by bank B is written on the back of the cheque, indemnifying the paying bank against any loss by paying the cheque.

In cases where one bank is the clearing agent of the second bank, then this is quite acceptable.

7 *Mutilation*: A cheque must be complete and regular. Any cheque that bears evidence of being mutilated or torn must be returned unpaid, unless a confirmation has been made by the collecting banker.

8 *Alteration*: Any alteration to a cheque must have the signature(s) of the drawer(s), although in practice, some banks will accept the initials of the drawer.

9 *Countermand of payment*: A customer has the right to stop payment of a cheque before presentation and payment of that cheque has been made. A bank must not pay such a cheque once notification has been received.

10 *Funds*: Customers should under normal circumstances have funds to meet the cheques drawn and presented for payment, otherwise they must contact the bank and agree that some overdraft or loan is given.

However, the practice has grown up that customers will anticipate their salary or other income and draw a cheque which creates an overdraft for which no authorization has been given. The bank may allow this, but should the situation seem to the bank to be continuing or becoming out of hand, the bank must contact the customer and regularize the position.

11 *Payment against a cheque card*: A bank agrees to honour a cheque, even when no funds are available, providing the cheque has been drawn under the conditions laid down. Should there be evidence that any rule has been broken (e.g.

the cheque is over £50), then the bank has the right, if necessary, to refuse payment.

12 *Receipts*: From time to time pension funds and insurance companies will issue cheques which require a receipt. This will be indicated by a large 'R' printed on the face of the cheque. In these cases the signature of the payee must be in the place indicated.

13 *Legal bar*: A legal bar is a situation where the law has imposed a stop on the account. It will happen when a person dies, or goes bankrupt, or a company goes into either voluntary or compulsory liquidation, or an individual is mentally incapable of controlling his own affairs. In each of the above cases the responsibility of the customer's affairs is vested in a trustee or executor. Until the appointment of such a person has been made, no funds must pass out of the account.

From time to time a court may order the freezing of an account either by a garnishee order or by an order of sequestration. When a bank receives either of these orders it must comply strictly with the instructions given.

A further legal bar will occur when an exchange control is imposed either generally or specifically. At the moment no exchange control regulation is in operation. But during the Falklands conflict sanctions were imposed on Argentina, so that funds transferred to an Argentinian citizen were illegal and payment would be refused by a bank. Similarly, when sanctions were imposed on Rhodesia payment without permission was not allowed.

Although the Exchange Control Act 1947 has been repealed, and one hopes that it will not be reimposed, a situation could arise where some form of control is brought back. Banks realize this and do keep records of 'external accounts'.

All this may seem a long ardous procedure, but in practice it takes very little time. A practised eye can soon see whether a cheque is in order or not. Stops and 'bad' accounts and other cautions are properly recorded, so that very few cases of negligence occur.

Procedure for non-payment

Should the occasion arise that a cheque, for any reason, is not going to be paid, then the answer is written on the cheque, usually in red, in the top left-hand corner. A debit entry on the collecting banker is passed through the clearing. Then an entry is made in an unpaids register, so that a record of the amount, name of customer, the collecting bank, and reason for non-payment, is kept for future reference. The unpaid cheque, with a printed note, is sent by first-class mail to the bank or branch specified in the crossing on the front of the cheque. The customer is also notified of the details of his cheque that has been unpaid, plus any charges to his account.

The collecting bank will on the fourth day receive the unpaid cheque in its morning post. On receipt, they will immediately debit the customer for the amount of the cheque and credit an unpaids account. The unpaid cheque could either be presented when the answer is, for example 'uncleared effects, please re-present' or 'post-dated cheque, please re-present'. Alternatively, the cheque could be returned to the customer if the answer is 'refer to drawer' or 'words and figures differ'. In all cases the customer must be notified (1) that the cheque is unpaid – for whatever reason – and (2) his account has been debited.

The credit on the unpaids account will be cleared by the claim made by the paying banker who when returning the cheque passed a claim through the clearing system.

From time to time a manager is involved in a situation whereby a cheque is received in the morning in clearing which he feels he cannot pay, and at the same time he does not want to damage his customer's creditworthiness by returning the cheque unpaid for lack of funds. In these circumstances he would normally contact the customer, advise him of the situation and ask whether a credit has been paid in at any other branch or bank to meet this cheque and perhaps any other cheques, or whether he could call in at the branch and rectify the position. Should this situation arise, it is customary for the paying banker to hold a decision to pay or to dishonour until midday the following business day. If the customer pays in cash or cleared funds to the credit of his account, and the cheque can be paid, then the matter will rest there, but should the customer not be able to meet the cheque, then by midday it is customary for the paying banker to contact the collecting banker, explain the circumstances to him and advise him that the cheque is being returned unpaid.

This procedure is adopted because the collecting bank is entitled to consider that after four days the credit to his customer's account which contained cheques presented for payment through the clearing system could be considered as paid, therefore his customer is entitled to withdraw his funds as and when required. In any case, under the rules of the CLSB, cheques should be returned unpaid by the close of business on the day of receipt, so if there is any breach of this regulation, some urgent action must be taken.

The credit clearing

This clearing system is part of the Cheque & Credit Clearing Co. Ltd, but you may recall that in earlier years credits paid in at either another branch or bank were sent onto the named bank and branch by post.

With the expansion in the use of computers and the growth in banking business, it became necessary for this area of operations to be streamlined and an efficient clearing process to be set up. In 1960 the credit transfer system was introduced. At first the process was rather slow, but as time went on, so the number of items processed through the credit clearing system grew. People began to realize that there was no need to send cheques to a variety of creditors, postal orders for small amounts were unnecessary and the creditors account could be credited without any fuss or fee.

At first, all credits that were sent to the clearing house were sorted by hand, but as the Magnetic Ink Character Recognition system (MICR) improved, so all credits contained the magnetic ink characters and are now sorted by computer. The system, now known as the Bank Giro system, is operated in exactly the same way as the cheque clearing system, except instead of debiting a customer, they are credited. It still takes three working days for any credit to go from one bank to another.

Truncation

At this point it is worth mentioning a system which is perhaps in its infancy. Truncation is a means of passing entries to the debit or credit of an account either in another branch or another bank without the movement of paper. It should be emphasized that the system is still relatively new, but the whole point is to assist the reduction in the movement of paper throughout the banking system. As we have seen in Table 2, the amount of cheques and credits passed daily through the clearing systems is enormous.

An example will help explain a truncation system. If I wished to draw money from another branch of the bank where my account is being held, then providing I have either my cheque card, an encashment facility or other arrangements have been made, then the agent branch will cash my cheque. This cheque, however, will not be sent to the drawee branch, but will be retained in the branch where the encashment was made. The details of my cheque and the amount will be transferred over the branch terminals to the debit of my account. My cheque will not be returned to me with my statement; indeed, it is now the practice not to give cheques to customers when despatching statements, except when instructions are given to the contrary. The same applies to credits, which can under certain circumstances be truncated, and unpaid claims on other branches have the same treatment. The truncation procedure does not apply to all banks, so you should examine your own banking system to see whether this is in operation.

CHAPS and town clearing

This is a clearing system that operates in the City of London only and for those banks that are part of the town clearing system. These include not only the banks of the general clearing but also Bank of Scotland, Citibank, Clydesdale Bank, Coutts & Co. and Standard Chartered. These banks will be identified by the fact that the branches within the City of London will have the letter 'T' beside their national code number, which can usually be seen on the top right-hand corner of a cheque.

The purpose of both these clearing systems is to ensure that the large payments between the financial institutions and markets in the City of London are cleared the same day. Large payments are those over £10,000.

THE TOWN CLEARING SYSTEM

In principle, the town clearing system works in the following way. Each working day the cheques that are paid in at the various city branches are sorted and those for the town clearing are sorted specially into the bundles for each of the other clearing banks. When the city branches close at 3 pm all the town clearing cheques are given priority and sorted, listed and bundled and taken by a messenger to the clearing house, re-sorted and despatched within minutes to the drawee bank. The cheques, bankers payments, bankers drafts, bills of exchange, and so on, are then paid, or if not paid, returned to the collecting bank by 4.45 pm.

THE CHAPS SYSTEM

The purpose of the CHAPS system (Clearing House Automated Payment System), is to enable funds to be transmitted quickly and efficiently from one bank to another within the City of London. The system is additional to the town clearing, but it should be emphasized that London being a major international financial centre, there must be a means of rapid transmission if London is to retain this position. The system did have a few 'labour pains' before it was finally put into operation in early 1980s.

The banks in the CHAPS system are known as settlement banks. These banks have the computer facilities to make and receive the necessary payments. For example, if a company has to make a large payment – say, £200,000 – to another company, and that payment must be made by a certain day, then assuming funds are available, the remitter will request his bank to remit the funds by means of a CHAPS payment.

It is assumed that (1) the beneficiary is an account holder of the receiving bank and (2) the receiving bank is a member of CHAPS. The procedure is as follows:

1. The bank will process the payment instruction internally.
2. It will compile a CHAPS payment with authentication.
3. This will be processed through the remitting banks 'Gateway', which will send the message via the British Telecom Switching Service. This message will be acknowledged and logged for audit and settlement purposes.
4. The receiving bank will receive the message, acknowledge and log the details for settlement and audit.
5. The message will be checked, the authentication will be confirmed, details of the account, amount, and so on, retained and placed on the beneficiary's account by the receiving bank's computer.
6. The customer will then be advised that his account has been credited and the following details given: the amount, remitter, value date, references.

SETTLEMENT

One can imagine the large volume of payments and amounts being passed through the Gateways of the various banks. It is therefore necessary to have some way of ascertaining how much is owed by one bank to another.

Each bank will keep a record of payments to and payments from a particular bank. To assist this reconciliation, each Gateway has a complete audit trail which can be used if any discrepancies arise and so any difference can be isolated and rectified. Second, the details of each payment are recorded in the Gateway and as each payment is executed, a running total can be checked as validation of receipt of payment. If there is a discrepancy, remedial action can be taken immediately.

On agreement on each day's business and the agreement between a pair of banks, the bank that owes the outstanding balance will send a CHAPS message to the Bank of England to transfer the amount owed to the bank to whom the balance is due.

OTHER USES OF CHAPS

Although it has been stated that CHAPS is used for payments to and from settlement banks in the City of London, the settlement banks and CHAPS can be used for:

1 Urgent payments received from abroad.
2 Telephonic requests from branches outside the town area to make urgent payment to branches of other banks outside the town area. The recipient bank will on receipt of funds advise the beneficiary branch by the quickest possible means.
3 Non-settlement banks wishing to pay same-day value funds to another bank.
4 Large corporate customers who wish to pay funds to another.

Bankers Automated Clearing Services Ltd (BACS)

This company has the following member banks: Bank of England, Barclays Bank, Bank of Scotland, Clydesdale Bank, Co-operative Bank, Coutts & Co., Central Trustee Savings Bank, Lloyds Bank, Midland Bank, National Girobank, National Westminster Bank and Royal Bank of Scotland.

Within a short time it is expected that the Abbey National and the Halifax building societies will be the first non-banks to join a clearing company, so that direct debits and standing orders of the customers of the two building societies will be processed directly into the banking system.

BACS performs the same function as any clearing department, except that it does not read the MICR numbers at the bottom of a cheque, but reads instructions from a magnetic tape. The importance of BACS is that transmission of funds is done without paper and that it can transmit either debits or credits, so that a branch of any member bank can, through its computer system, notify BACS of its standing-order payments in advance, so that on the due date the debiting of the bank/customer is made and the crediting of the various creditors is done at the same time.

Very many employees of large companies, government departments, and so on, are paid their salaries in this way.

The organization will transmit to BACS its authenicated authority to credit its employees with a variety of amounts at a variety of banks and branches. BACS has authority to debit the remitter's account for the total of the payments made. By this method the employees are assured that funds are available on their account on the due date, and the paperwork involved in this operation is almost eliminated. By the same token, companies involved in the direct-debit system can pass one credit to their bank account, and any number of debits to the accounts of their various customers. In this way they are assured of good money on a due date and the administration is reduced. Settlement is made through the Bank of England in the usual way.

Electronic Funds Transfer at Point of Sale (EFT-POS)

EFT-POS is a method whereby a person buying goods in a retail environment is able to hand his 'plastic card' (credit card, debit or ATM card, charge card or in-store card) to the cashier. The cashier passes the card through the EPT-POS terminal, which captures the electronic information contained within the magnetic stripe, and this, together with the amount, is then used to debit the consumer's account and credit the retailer's account.

HISTORY

Since this method of debt settlement is not yet fully operational but likely to become operative in the not too distant future, it is worthwhile looking at its brief history. In the 1970s it became increasingly obvious to the banks that with the spread of consumer banking, pressure on the existing paper-based debit and credit clearings would occur.

Unfortunately, the technology was not available at that time to introduce such a system and, although major advances arising from the use of new technology were seen, including the introduction of BACS and CHAPS, it was not until 1980s that banks began looking at EFT-POS as a practical solution.

This led to the announcement by the Committee of London and Scottish Banks (CLSB) – at that time known as the Committee of London Clearing Banks – in which all the major banks reaffirmed their commitment to the development of EFT-POS.

To achieve this commitment a development company, EFT-POS Administration Ltd, was set up under the auspices of the CLSB, with the initial costs being met by the CLSB participant banks. EFT-POS Administration Ltd's role was to liaise with banks, equipment manufacturers and retailers to ascertain requirements for an EFT-POS system, and from that position commence the process of reaching an agreement on system standards (e.g. mode of operation, security requirements, cost, and so on), and then to take forward its implementation. However, in 1982 Clydesdale Bank had commenced a pilot exercise and in 1983 Cresta Communications Ltd, in conjunction with British Telecom, commenced an EFT-POS service which accepted a number of charge and credit cards.

Due to these existing initiatives it was felt that it would be worthwhile to commence a number of additional pilot schemes to show their commitment in a practical manner and to gain advance experience, which would be shared with the CLSB. To this end, a number of experimental projects are now in existence, but before considering these it would be worthwhile looking at the proposed method of operation and benefits to all parties following the installation of EFT-POS.

OPERATION AND BENEFITS

A customer hands his card to the cashier, who will pass it through a card-reader, where the information on the magnetic stripe (contained on the back of virtually all plastic cards presently in issue) is read. This this is known as 'wiping'.

The card-holder then either enters his personal identification number (PIN) or signs; and the amount, card details and PIN (where required) are then 'encrypted' (which is a means of electronically scrambling information) and then sent for checking, if full authorization is required. If the transaction is below any agreed 'floor limit' it is stored electronically for later transmission in batch. Providing there are sufficient available funds and the card is not stolen or badly misused by the card-holder, the transaction is authorized within a maximum thirty-second timescale.

A receipt is then printed and the customer's account debited and the retailer's account credited the next day or, alternatively, a day or two later, depending upon the type of individual arrangement in use. The basic EFT-POS network structure consists, therefore, of a retailer terminal which, using British Telecom lines and a data network, links the terminal equipment with the computers of the banks and other organizations holding the retailers' and customers' accounts.

As to the benefits of EFT-POS, these should accrue to all parties.

The retailer
He can expect to gain immediately the following benefits:

1 Speed
   - Next-day crediting of his account, which will either ease cash flow (reduce interest costs) or make funds available earlier for deposit.
   - A faster in-store checkout together with the simplification of procedures at the point of sale, particularly in comparison with existing cheque/credit card procedures.
2 Guaranteed funds, which will not be restricted to the existing cheque card limit of £50.
3 Less paper handling, quite simply by reducing the volumes of cheques issued.
4 Greater security, by the reduction in cash holdings.
5 Other benefits – for example:
   - Using the system for management information.
   - Staff costs may be reduced due to the removal of 'back office processing'.
   - The containment of bank charges.
   - Other ancillary services which may be offered along with the system by the bank sponsor.

The customer
The benefits for the 'man in the street' will be:

1 The convenience and flexibility arising from this additional payment method.
2 Speed – the ability to purchase and leave immediately with high-value goods without the constraint of the cheque card limit of £50 and no need to feel embarrassed at causing delays in stores due to writing cheques, waiting for credit card authorization, and so on.
3 Less risk – as there will be no need to carry bulky cheque books, the customer will not need to fear the loss of such items or loss of cash, etc.
4 Costs – following the introduction of this service the customers can expect bank charges to be contained through the introduction of these automatic entries.

Banks

The benefits for the banks are:

1 Reduction in paper volume – it is anticipated that clearing costs will be contained and eventually reduced following the introduction of EFT-POS.
2 Reduction of fraud – due to the nature of the system, a card can be blocked electronically as soon as its loss is reported.

It must be appreciated that EFT-POS is an alternative payment method and *not* a replacement of cash and cheques, i.e. the customer has the option of choosing the payment method used.

EFT-POS IN THE UK

A number of different EFT-POS schemes are presently in operation within the UK and a brief résumé of those involved is detailed in Table 4. As can be seen there is substantial activity within this field by the major banks and, without doubt, more will be seen within the next couple of years.

NATIONAL WESTMINSTER BANK GROUP: STREAMLINE

For purposes of this book, National Westminster have consented to make available the following details.

Table 4 EFT–POS schemes in the UK

System	Sponsoring institutions	Cards accepted	Terminals and outlets	Mode of operation
Counterplus (start-up February 1982)	Clydesdale Bank	Clydesdale's Autobank cards (700,000 in issue); Midland Bank Group ATM and NatWest Access cards; MasterCard Gold from Midland	33 terminals, 29 outlets (mainly BP petrol stations but one superstore) in W. Scotland, Glasgow and Aberdeen	On-line authorization. Data forwarded in batch mode via on-line link to central computer
Cresta Communications	Cresta and British Telecom	Amex, Diners, Visa, Access, MasterCard, THF Gold Card	'Several hundred' (outlets include Heron petrol stations, C&A stores, Argos stores, Trust House Forte hotels	On-line authorization check against blacklist held by British Telecom. On-line data transfer to British Telecom, forward on- or off-line.
PISCES (start-up September 1984)	System operated by Centre-file (data-processing subsidiary of NatWest	Access, Diners, Amex, Visa, Esso charge card	475 petrol stations with one terminal each	Off-line data capture telephone authorization if over line by Centre-file at night
PayPoint (start-up October 1985)	Anglia Building Society	Angliacard (50,000 issued)	171 terminals, 109 outlets in Northampton	On-line, real-time authorization and data transfer
Speedline (start-up February 1986)	Midland Bank	Midland Group ATM cards; NatWest Group ATM cards; all Access credit cards; MasterCard Gold card from Midland Bank	15 outlets – C&A Modes; Clockhouse; Dolcis; Freeman, Hardy & Willis; H. Samuel; Olympus; Thomas Cook; BP	On-line check against £200 weekly card withdrawal limit at controller. Data transferred to Midland centre in batch mode for next-day settlement

Streamline (start-up April 1986)	NatWest Group	NatWest Group ATM cards and Midland ATM cards, plus Access and Visa credit cards and Diners and Amex charge cards; NatWest and Midland Gold Cards	24 – Texaco and Mobil petrol stations	Off-line authorization. Card checked against negative files in terminal, updated every night by Centre-file. Centre-file pick up transactions in batch mode as per PISCES
DARTS (end of March 1986)	Barclaycard	Barclaycard (Visa), Access	80 terminals mainly at Brent Cross shopping centre, but also 50 at Heathrow airport and 28 at Fortnum & Mason in London	On-line authorization coupled with visual signature verification. Data stored on tape and sent in batch mode to credit card companies
ACCEPT (start-up, late 1986)	Access	Access (MasterCard), Visa	To begin in Romford	On-line authorization coupled with visual signature verification. Data stored on tape and sent in batch mode to credit card companies

Operation

Essentially, the streamline experiment places the ATM card bases of the NatWest Group and the Midland Group (via separate reciprocity agreements) in a retail environment for the first time using PIN verification. Access cards of NatWest, Midland and Lloyds can also be used with PIN verification or signature as well as NatWest and Midland Gold Cards. The Streamline equipment will also accept a very wide range of other cards (e.g. Barclaycard) which are signature-based still using electronic data capture.

The Streamline system operates using Centre-file's highly successful PISCES (Petroleum Industry Service for the Clearance, Electronically, of Sales) scheme, which connects to the terminal during British Telecom's Midnight Window (12.00 midnight to 6 am) and the transaction information is collected and sorted by Centre-file and passed on to the appropriate card-issuers. Customers' accounts are debited a day or so after the transaction has occurred.

Sites

A test site was installed in February 1986 at Sawbridgeworth and, following successful completion of testing, the experiment was 'rolled out' to the Texaco Thames Valley and Mobil Sheffield sites. Following installation, which occurred in mid-March 1986, all sites were immediately made available for public use. Streamline was launched formally at the ten Texaco service stations sited along the 'western corridor' from West London to Reading, on Tuesday 21 April 1986 and at the fifteen Mobil sites in and around the Sheffield area on 29 April 1986.

Research and monitoring

In the NatWest experiment they are seeing transaction values for ATM card usage averaging £25,000 per week. Total Streamline usage, including credit card transactions, amount to approximately £140,000 per week.

These figures suggest a favourable response from ATM card-holders, and the petrol partners in the experiment are impressed by the take-up and the ancillary benefits, such as speed of transaction, guaranteed funds, savings in staff time, and so on.

SUMMARY

This is a very new and exciting area. We can expect to see substantial changes occurring within the next decade which will lead eventually to the installation of EFT-POS equipment in virtually every retailer's store.

Self-examination questions

1 What do the letters CLSB and APACS mean?
2 Name the banks that are members of the Cheque and Credit Clearing Co. Ltd.
3 Describe the process for the payment of a cheque from the day it is presented for credit to the account of the customer until final payment.
4 How are inter-bank clearing differences settled?
5 When a cheque is paid by the paying banker, state the points he would examine on the cheque before final payment.
6 Under which situations would the law prevent payment of a cheque.
7 When there is non-payment of a cheque, for any reason, what procedure is adopted by the paying banker?
8 Describe the CHAPS and town clearing system.
9 What do the letters EFT-POS mean?
10 Describe the advantages of using the EFT-POS system from the point of view of 'the man in the street'.

11 Control of the banking system

In Chapters 1 to 3 we discussed how the banks evolved, in particular how the Bank of England was established in 1694, because it had the confidence of the sovereign, the government and, for that time, a large capital base – far greater than that of its competitors, the private banks. It was from its first days the leading bank in the country. Very gradually and over a long time it was given certain functions so that it could act as a central bank, banker to the government and the banker to other banks. This is still true today and now includes a role in advising the government of the day on matters of international finance, money supply, economic trends, and so on, and is responsible for licensing banks and other deposit-taking institutions and for their regular supervision.

However, one of its most important roles of the Bank of England is the control of the banking system. In order to better understand the present, let us know take a look at the past.

Pre-1971

For more than two centuries the Bank of England has been primarily responsible for the control of the banking system. One method was by the maintenance of the Bank Rate. This was the rate of interest that was charged to the various discount houses that went to the Bank of England to borrow funds to balance their books. The discount houses went to the Bank of England to borrow money because at that particular time they were unable to borrow from the various banks in London, who at that moment were not in a position to lend. As the lender of last resort, the Bank of England would lend as much money as was required by the discount houses. This rate of interest was announced each Thursday afternoon, by a notice being displayed in the entrance hall of the Bank of England. Any changes immediately affected the lending rates and deposit rates of the banks. During periods of crisis the rate could be, and was, changed on other days.

In the nineteenth and early twentieth century the banking system consisted mainly of merchant banks, British Commonwealth banks, clearing banks, private banks and a few foreign banks. The clearing banks set the pattern of behaviour and were the most influential. In fact, there were mutual agreements between these banks to offer the same services for the same charge. Interest rates on deposit accounts were the same, as was the interest charged on overdrafts and loans.

Besides this cartel, the Bank of England insisted that all banks keep a cash ratio of 8 per cent. That is 8 per cent of their deposits must be kept either in cash in tills or in an account with the central bank. In addition to this, a liquidity ratio of 28 per cent had to be maintained. This liquidity ratio meant that as well as 8 per cent being locked up in non-interest-bearing accounts or kept in cash form, the other 20 per cent had to be loaned out to the various discount houses or used to purchase short-term government stock or Treasury bills.

By these means the Bank was able to control the money supply and the banking system, so that if there was a need to reduce the amount of cash in circulation, there would be, for example, an increase in the sale of government stock. The public would purchase this stock, which meant that funds would be paid to the Bank from the bank accounts of individuals and firms. This would reduce the amount of funds held by banks for their customers, so that any reduction in the total deposits held, must also reduce the amount held in cash or the Bank of England, to the 8 per cent. Also, the liquidity amount must be reduced to the required 28 per cent, and finally, because of the reduction in deposits, there would also be a reduction in the total amount advanced.

The same principle would apply when the Inland Revenue demanded payment of taxes in June/July for the previous financial year. Payments were made from the bank accounts of companies, traders and individuals to the Inland Revenue, who paid these cheques into their account at the Bank of

England. This meant that the balances of the individual banks at the Bank of England were reduced to meet these cheques, and so were the balances of the customers who drew them. With reduced deposits the banks had to adjust their cash to a new level which would equal 8 per cent of their deposits, and a new liquidity amount which would equal 28 per cent of the deposits. These adjustments were made regularly, to conform to the movements of the supply and demand of money and credit.

At this time the Bank of England had no legal powers to compel any bank to comply with this liquidity formula, but because it was traditional for banks to listen to the central bank, all banks complied without question.

In the same way, the Bank from time to time issued directives. These directives covered a variety of instructions, but dealt with particularly, the quantitative and qualitative lending positions of banks. Qualitative lending directives meant that banks were told which professions, trades and industries they should lend to and those that they should not lend to. Even today the branches of banks will send in regular returns to their head office, specifying which classes of individuals, trades, professions, industries are borrowing funds. No names are given, just amounts. These branch returns are collated and one return sent to the Bank of England showing the amounts advanced to various classifications. Quantitative lending directives informed banks that they may lend to whom they please, but advised them of the maximum any bank could globally lend in a stated period. The banks did not like this restriction of their freedom, but they complied. Tradition in the City of London is strong and these loose ties between institutions were some of the factors that made London the major financial centre of the world.

While the number of banks in the UK were small, the control of the banking system was relatively easy, particularly soon after the Second World War, when funds could not be easily transferred out of the country and any foreign remittances received had to be paid into a bank. Rates of exchange were fixed. Interest rates did not move as frequently as they do now, nor was the banking habit as widespread as it is today.

Control of the banking system 165

All this changed in the early 1960s, when exchange control regulations were relaxed, and due to the demand for international capital, London because of its tradition, reputation and ease of communication, became the centre of foreign-exchange transactions and the centre of the Eurocurrency market. Both these markets attracted foreign banks to London.

As banks could open up offices in London without any formality; there were about thirty or more banks opening up each year either as representative offices or full branches. At present there are now over 400 foreign banks in London, all involved in both the foreign-exchange and Eurocurrency markets.

With these banks arriving in London, without knowledge of the traditions of London they did not participate in the banks' cartel and went out to obtain whatever business they could obtain – often offering services at a commission below that taken by the major London banks. There marketing tactics were more aggressive than those employed by domestic branch managers. In fact, it is difficult to imagine that in the days of the older generation, bank managers did not market services, they waited for customers to come to the bank. They had no need to visit factories, shops, warehouses and industrial sites. They expected to sit in their offices and transact business from there.

1971–81

To overcome this situation and allow competition between all banks, and at the same time involve banks in maintaining control of credit, the Bank of England in May 1971 introduced a discussion paper called 'Competition and Credit Control'. This paper set out a new system designed to encourage freer competition between banks and give the authorities less control of credit. The control of credit would be in the hands of the market itself. All banks were included in the scheme, and also the discount market would bid for Treasury bills rather than have an agreed price to be paid. The points covered by the paper and implemented were as follows:

1 Banks and discount houses would abandon their mutual agreements of interest rates so as to allow freer competition.

2 The quantitative directives to banks would end.

3 Bank overdraft rates, loan rates and interest rates would no longer be linked to the Bank Rate, but each bank would calculate their own rates of interest by relating them to its own 'base rate'. This rate they could vary as they wished.

4 Banks would no longer have to keep a 28 per cent liquidity ratio, nor would there be a need for an 8 per cent cash ratio; all banks would keep a minimum of 12.5 per cent of the eligible liabilities in reserve assets. 'Eligible liabilities' was nothing more than the new name for deposits, but according to a strict definition they did not include any deposits which had a maturity of over two years. 'Reserve assets' were defined as those funds with the Bank of England, Treasury Bills, money at call with the London Money Market. Cash in tills was not included as a reserve asset.

5 All financial institutions with liabilities of £10 million or more must keep 0.5 per cent of their eligible liabilities with the Bank of England. These funds did not earn any interest and the amount would be adjusted twice a year to be in line with the average amount of eligible liabilities held. Clearing banks would be expected to hold balances on other accounts with balances as appropriate for settlement of inter-bank clearing differences.

6 The Minimum Lending Rate (MLR) would replace the Bank Rate. The MLR would be calculated at the average rate of discount for Treasury bills plus 0.5 per cent rounded up to the nearest quarter per cent above. For example, supposing the average rate of discounting Treasury bills were 9.876 per cent, then adding 0.5 per cent would make it 10.376 per cent; rounding this figure upwards to the nearest quarter per cent, the MLR for that week would be 10.5 per cent.

Clearly, with the liquidity reduced from 28 per cent to

12.5 per cent, the banks would have more money to lend. This was the case. A new form of lending was introduced, first by Midland Bank, and quickly followed by the others: personal loans. At that time it meant that any person could walk into a bank, give a reason for wishing to borrow – no matter how vague – and he or she would be able to borrow, even if that person had no account or previous connections with the bank. At the other end of the market, banks merchant, secondary, foreign, and so on, were all lending money for what one these days would consider speculation on the property market, foreign-exchange market, stock market, commodities market, and so on. Speculation was in the air. Inflation was high and many people made fortunes in the period from 1972 to 1974.

This could not continue and when it was realized that this was nothing more than a bubble, banks either reduced their lending or called in the advances given. Of course, many companies could not repay. They relied on speculative profits. As funds were not forthcoming, the companies were liquidated. However, the banks borrowing short and lending long, found that they themselves could not meet their commitments and so either went into liquidation or appealed to the Bank of England to give them assistance.

To a large number of banks, the Bank of England launched 'the lifeboat'. This was the name given to assistance given by either the Bank of England itself, or at their request the assistance given by the major banks. These smaller banks were saved either by the injection of a massive amount of capital or the introduction of senior management to take control, or a combination of both methods. Sadly, many banks went into liquidation and their names have disappeared from banking.

This was not a good period for the banking industry. In due time, 'special deposits' were introduced, and indeed, to maintain even stricter control, 'supplementary special deposits' (nicknamed 'The Corset') were imposed. This meant that a percentage of deposits had to be retained on a special-deposit account with the central bank; in consequence, lending was further reduced.

Banking Act 1979

For nearly three hundred years this country, one of the most advanced industrialized countries in the world, a leader in world trade and its capital as a leading financial centre, had no statutory legislation governing its banking system. It relied on, quite successfully, the co-operation of institutions that comprised the financial markets and the informal influence of the Bank of England.

Of course, over the years there has been legislation relevant to banks and other financial institutions. Such Acts include, Bills of Exchange Act (1882), Moneylenders Act (1927), Protection of Depositors Act (1963), Exchange Control Act (1947) and, of course, the Consumer Credit Act (1974).

The reasons for the introduction for the first Act of Parliament which had direct influence and control of the banking system were as follows:

1 Following the banking crisis of 1972–4, it was necessary to maintain greater control and supervision over the banking system, particularly the smaller institutions.
2 There was confusion in the mind of the general public as to what was and what was not a bank.
3 The major banks were not just domestic institutions but were large international organizations as well.
4 It was necessary to have statutory control of the banking systems in order to comply with the objectives laid down by the EEC.

The purpose of the Banking Act can be stated as follows:

1 To prevent any bank or financial institution, whether existing or newly formed, from accepting deposits without obtaining authority to do so from the Bank of England. A deposit for the purposes of this Act are funds transferred to those institutions whose everyday business is to take in deposits. A hotelier who accepts deposits from persons who wish to reserve accommodation for a week or fortnight, need not apply to the Bank of England for authority, as his main business is not in accepting deposits but offering food, shelter and accommodation. In the same way, an estate agent is not a

deposit taker, because his main trade is the buying and selling of property. The acceptance of money as consideration for a contract is only incidental to the business itself and not the main purpose.

2 To lay down the criteria which must be satisfied if such authority is given; the applicant must satisfy the Bank of England in the following areas:

(a) New deposit-taking companies must commence business with a minimum capital of £250,000 and recognized banks with a minimum capital of £5 million. There is a White Paper before Parliament recommending that, amongst other matters, the two different types of deposit institutions should disappear and a minimum capital should be £1 million for all. This is not likely to become law until the end of 1987.
(b) Competent management – on this point very little has been provided, but it would appear that the Bank of England would rely on its own knowledge of the applicant, its senior management either at home or abroad. No doubt such information on a foreign bank could be obtained from the central bank of the country concerned.
(c) Wide range of banking services – the Act lays down five services required by a bank, of which only the first two are compulsory, but any bank of repute will probably offer all the services stated. They are:
    - acceptance of deposits
    - granting of loans
    - foreign exchange transactions
    - the provision of bill finance and handling of documentation for foreign trade
    - investment management and corporate finance facilities.
(d) Have a good standing and reputation in the financial community – it is most unusual for a bank to be formed from a vacuum; normally, it will grow from some other institution or be an established bank from another country.

3 To provide statutory authority for the supervision by the Bank of England of the activities of all such institutions: This indicates quite categorically that the Bank of England no longer has to rely on 'persuasion' for compliance with its directives. It could, if necessary, penalize any institution that refuses to comply with a request. However, having said that, the major banks are in regular consultation at all levels with the Bank of England and would offer any advice and co-operation to ensure that there are orderly financial markets, and the needs of the country are uppermost. The need for supervision was reinforced in the recent past when Johnson Matthey (Bankers) Ltd needed support.

4 To control the use of banking names and descriptions limiting them to banks: With the proposed merger of the two types of financial institution, this is likely to be amended in the next bill presented to Parliament.

5 To provide a measure of protection for depositers through the medium of a Depositors Protection Fund: In the event of a collapse of a bank of deposit-taking institution, a depositor can receive up to a maximum of 75 per cent of his deposit of £10,000 – that is, the maximum a depositor is likely to receive in such an event is £7,500.

CONCLUSION

The Banking Act 1979 provides a very comprehensive framework for the Bank of England to control the activities of the deposit-taking institutions. At the same time, it does not prevent the use of existing legislation, such as the Prevention of Fraud (Investment) Act 1958 and the Consumer Credit Act 1974.

The supervision of banks changes to meet the needs of the day. Amongst these matters is the importance of liquidity, and it is now necessary for each institution to satisfy the Bank that its liquidity is adequate.

A White Paper published in December 1985 on banking supervision, is, at the time of writing, before Parliament.

Control of the banking system

1981 onwards

The MLR was suspended in August 1981 and up to the time of writing, with the exception of one day, has not been restored. In its place new arrangements have been adopted by the Bank of England to ensure the adequacy of liquidity in the banking sector and to influence the interest rates, not by an MLR, but through open-market operations – the buying and selling eligible bills of exchange – and not by lending directly to the discount houses.

The present method of supervision is to make the market in Treasury bills and commercial bills large enough to influence interest rates. To effect this, the previous small group of 'good names' has been increased to over a hundred banks who have now 'eligible status'. This means that they are first-class banks – members of the Acceptance Houses Committee, clearing banks, Commonwealth banks, some foreign banks, whose names on bills are acceptable for rediscount at the Bank of England and therefore attract the finest interest rates.

To become an 'eligible' bank the following criteria must be met:

1 The applicant must have and maintain a broadly based, substantial acceptance business in the UK.
2 Its acceptances must command the finest rates in the markets for ineligible bills.
3 In the case of foreign banks, British banks must enjoy reciprocal opportunities in the foreign owners' domestic market.

Banks that were granted this status undertook to abide by certain conditions:

1 To maintain 5 per cent of eligible liabilities on a secured basis with members of the London Discount Market Association (LDMA) and/or with money brokers and gilt-edged jobbers.
2 To ensure that the minimum on any one day does not fall below 2.5 per cent of eligible liabilities.
3 All institutions with eligible liabilities of £10 million or more will keep 0.5 per cent on a non-operational, non-interest-earning account with the Bank of England.

In the event of a cash shortage, the Bank will inform the discount houses that they will be prepared to buy eligible bills in the following maturity bands. The interest rates charged are not known in advance:

Band 1   1–14 days
Band 2   15–33 days
Band 3   34–63 days
Band 4   64–91 days

From time to time the Bank will agree to buy longer-term dated bills.

OTHER FORMS OF SUPERVISION

As you have just read, the main methods of supervising the banking system is by the authorization required by any institution that wishes to establish itself as a bank. This authority can be refused or given by the Bank of England under the Banking Act 1979. In order to ensure that banks maintain adequate liquidity, the Bank, under the same Act and the powers vested in it by the Bank of England Nationalization Act 1946, can demand various returns to ensure that no bank is acting in a way contrary to the guidelines laid down by the central bank.

As lender of last resort, the Bank of England can control the money supply and interest rates, which very quickly have an effect on the activities of all banks. Other methods that can be used, but may not necessarily be in use at the present moment are as follows.

Direct controls

These controls take the form of issuing directives to banks on lending which may be those of a quantitative nature, which places a limit on bank lending, thereby restricting the growth of deposits, which in turn influences the money supply. Qualitative controls involve the Bank of England advising banks which persons, businesses and industries they may lend to, or may not lend any further funds to, or must restrict lending to.

These directives, although seemingly of a dictatorial nature, are not so in practice. Prior to such directives being issued, discussions with the Treasury and meetings with bank directors and bank representatives will have taken place, so that when they are finally circulated, there will be the maximum co-operation with the authorities.

Reserve requirements

As we have seen, all banks are required to maintain a certain proportion of their eligible liabilities either in cash or liquid assets. This is often a prudent measure to ensure that there is adequate liquidity, but in order to control the money supply this percentage can either increase or decrease the ratio of cash or liquid assets, so that there will be an effect on the money supply.

Open-market operations

At any time the Bank of England can intervene in any of the financial markets. It will, for example, often enter the foreign-exchange markets, either as a buyer or seller of sterling, in order to adjust violent movements in the rate of exchange. It will purchase or sell government stock in order to affect liquidity.

Special deposits

For some years now this method of control has not been used, but if it was thought necessary to reinstitute this, then the central bank would do so without hesitation. All banks are requested to deposit a certain percentage of the eligible liabilities – that is make a special deposit – with the Bank of England; although it earns them a rate of interest, it reduces the amount available for investment in other liquid assets or for lending to customers.

CONCLUSION

The Bank of England, as the arm of the Treasury and the centre of all financial activity, has a responsibility to maintain economic and financial stability in the country as well as to adhere to the broad policies imposed upon it by the government. In order to carry out its function effectively, it is, by the very nature of things, considered to be a tolerant dictator. It can, in the final analysis, impose any constraint on any individual bank, to the point of refusing to allow it to operate in this country. It can also impose constraints on the banking system as a whole.

The effect of the measures imposed by the Bank of England, particularly those which increase or decrease interest rates, will sooner or later affect each one of us, whether we are borrowers, savers or investors. None of us that use money can escape.

Self-examination questions

1 Pre-1971, were there any differences between the various clearing banks in the rates of interest (a) offered on deposit account and (b) taken on advances?
2 State some of the cartel agreements that would disappear under 'Competition and Credit Control'.
3 (a) What are eligible liabilities? (b) What are reserve assets?
4 Do the letters MLR mean:
   (a) Maximum Lending Rate
   (b) Material Loan Rate
   (c) Minimum Lending Rate.
5 Describe the effect the increased liquidity had on the country after the introduction of paper 'Competition and Credit Control'.
6 State the reasons for the introduction of the Banking Act 1979.
7 State the criteria that must be satisfied before an institution is allowed to accept deposits.
8 What is an 'eligible bank'?
9 What do you understand by (a) quantitative directives and (b) qualitative directives?
10 What are open-market operations?

12 Banks and competition

So far we have dealt with banks and their involvement with the public at large. As we have said, there are over 400 banks all competing for business, all wanting to get a greater slice of the banking cake. All make profits each year. Yet within the UK there are other institutions, not banks, competing against banks and against each other to obtain the deposits from persons, businesses and other organizations.

Who are these organizations and what do they do? First let us look at those businesses and markets that compete for the funds of medium-sized and large businesses.

Competition for company deposits

OTHER COMPANIES

It is quite likely that when a limited company has a surplus of funds and feels that it is necessary for expansion to take over another company, then it will utilize those funds, and even borrow funds to buy out the shareholders or a competitor or a supplier of goods. This can happen in banking. As we have seen, Barclays took over Martins Bank, while fairly recently there was an unsuccessful attempt at a takeover of Standard Chartered Bank by Lloyds Bank.

While the takeover of a company by another may suit some organizations, it is often useful merely to have a share in the capital of a company as an investment, either to influence the company's trading policies or for a profit motive. In both cases, funds are extracted from the bank account and used elsewhere.

TREASURY BILLS

These are negotiable bills issued by the Bank of England on behalf of the Treasury. They normally have a life of ninety-one days and are issued at a discount – that is, at an amount below face value. The minimum value of such a bill is £5,000. When the bill matures they are presented to the Bank of England, who will pay the holder the face value of the bill.

These bills do not attract a rate of interest, but as already stated, they are issued at a discount, so it is possible to calculate the interest that can be received on purchase. For example, should a company purchase a bill with a face value of £50,000 for only £49,000, they would ninety-one days later make a profit of £1,000. This would be the equivalent of interest of 8 per cent per annum.

Treasury bills are useful for those who have funds available for a short term only. Rather than keeping these funds on a current account, Treasury bills can be purchased, thereby obtaining interest. Should the holder require these funds urgently, the bill can very quickly and easily be sold in the money market. They are safe, risk-free and liquid.

CERTIFICATES OF DEPOSIT

While a bank may have the account of a customer, other banks may attract funds away from that bank by offering deposits on more attractive terms.

A certificate of deposit is a fully negotiable instrument which can be transferred by the holder to another with the minimum of fuss and procedure. A deposit must be for a minimum of three months but could be up to five years. The bank receiving the deposit will issue a certificate stating the interest that the deposit attracts, the face value of the certificate and the date of maturity. Again, the holder can retain the certificate until maturity then obtain payment of the capital and interest. Alternatively, should he or she require funds during the life of the certificate, it can be sold on the money market and so the capital obtained plus some element of interest.

THE INTER-COMPANY MARKET

This market came into being in the late 1960s, when the Bank of England issued strict directives to banks on lending. This squeeze on lending meant that borrowers had to pay a high interest for borrowing, while those companies with funds could not obtain a high interest for surplus funds.

To take the place of banks the companies with funds to spare obtained the services of brokers who were able to arrange a loan between a lending company and a borrowing company. These loans were generally for a minimum of £50,000 and could range from three months to five years and, if necessary, beyond. Bank guarantees were often used to satisfy the security aspect of the borrowing.

GILT-EDGED STOCK

Gilt-edged stock is the name given to stock issued by the government and local authorities. It is called gilt-edged because before the Second World War the certificates were edged in gold paint. The purchase of government stock attracts interest at the going market rate and is easily purchased from a broker, and if funds are needed, can be sold back to a broker. Interest is paid twice-yearly, and the capital is repayable at maturity.

The purchaser of gilt-edged stock must be aware that the price might increase and decrease, not only with supply and demand, but with the fluctuation of market interest rates. Should market interest rates fall, then the current gilt-edged stock will rise in price. Should market interest rates rise, then it is likely that the capital value of the stock will fall.

SELF-INVESTMENT

The most favoured form of utilization of funds by a company is investment in itself. Obviously, the purchase of fixed assets to assist future expansion will be attractive when such assets are needed. The purchase of additional raw materials to turn into finished goods, when there is a demand for those goods, must be profitable. For retailers, the purchase of finished goods to meet current demands should be profitable and the best way of utilizing available funds.

Competition for company borrowing

Companies not only lend funds sometimes; they require funds. Then they may go to a bank and borrow money either by way of an overdraft or loan, giving the bank a debenture or some other form of security. But is this the cheapest method of borrowing? This depends on the market situation.

Banks must therefore compete in their lending services. As explained above, the inter-company market is not only a market where a company can lend its surplus funds, but should funds be required, then this is an alternative source of supply. Additionally, companies must also consider the following methods of borrowing.

SECURED OR UNSECURED LOANS

Should the company be public, then it is possible for it to raise either a secured or unsecured loan through the medium of the Stock Exchange. That is a prospectus could be issued and either large institutions, pension funds, insurance companies, and so on, could take part of a mortgage debenture (secured loan) or a naked debenture (unsecured loan), so that with the help of various organizations the company can raise a loan for a given period at a stated annual percentage rate, for a given amount and redeemed at a stated time. This could be cheaper than raising a loan from a bank. For the private company, it is quite possible for funds to be obtained from private sources, so that either one, two or more persons could make a similar loan to a company.

EURO-BOND LOANS

Should the company be fairly large and require not only funds but foreign currency as well, it is just as easy for it to obtain a borrowing say in US dollars, German marks, Swiss francs or any other major international currency. This form of borrowing is particularly useful for a company that intends to invest funds abroad, and will receive foreign-currency earnings, so that the currency loan will be repaid by its currency earnings. This is often a very attractive method of borrowing. To verify this situation, look at the borrowings of any major UK bank. They often borrow in the major currencies of the world. All major banks are particularly keen to assist any company to borrow currency.

RIGHTS ISSUES

Companies that need funds for expansion or for specific projects may, if necessary, call upon their shareholders to supply the necessary funds by offering them additional shares at an attractive price. For example, if the price of a £1 share in XYZ PLC stood at £2, then the offer of one share at £1.50 for every share held would be attractive to the ordinary shareholder, particularly if the dividends are good and the price of the share is rising steadily in the market. This way the company is raising the funds it requires easily and possibly without too much expense.

Competition for deposits from individuals

For individuals the range of places to deposit funds and to borrow money, other than banks, is far greater than those available to a company. It seems that every time one looks at a newspaper, particularly on a Saturday or Sunday, there are numerous advertisements and inducements to the public to invest money in all sorts of enterprises. Not only that, for those who are in desperate need of funds and do not understand the money markets, there are quite a lot of advertisements offering unsecured loans from £50 to £5,000. The financial pages of the national newspapers are quite bewildering and need careful study before taking any action. The various sources of depositing and borrowing funds for the individual are as follows:

BUILDING SOCIETIES

By far the most serious competitors to banks are the building societies. The basic function of a building society is to attract funds and use these funds to lend to others for the provision of loans for domestic house purchase, using the deeds as security for the loan.

Building societies are in theory non-profit-making organizations. They attract deposits by offering interest to the depositors and offer loans at higher interest rates. The differential between the lending rates and the borrowing rates pays all the expenses of the society.

Nearly all building societies are members of the Building Societies Association, which imposes certain conditions on its members with particular regard to liquidity, interest rates, and so on. The Chief Registrar of Friendly Societies is to the building societies what the Bank of England is to banks. The Chief Registrar has the power to investigate the affairs of a building society, control the advertising for funds, and so on.

Basically, building societies can be divided into three groups:

1 There are those that operate in a particular locality and have perhaps only one or two offices. These very small building societies attract funds from persons in the area and lend for house purchase in that area. The services offered are not as great as those of the larger building societies.

2 Those building societies that operate on a region or county may have offices in many towns and villages in the particular area. Their influence and reputation is well known and their services are somewhat greater than those in the first group. In recent years many of the building societies have expanded to move into the next group.

3 This group contains the major national building societies which have branches throughout the country. Usually their names do not indicate that they are of national importance – for example, Woolwich Building Society, Bradford & Bingley – but have retained their original names. The services they offer are expanding year by year.

All building societies offer depositors accounts which vary in only minor detail, but all the building societies have one thing in common: all accounts, whatever they are called, offer interest to the depositor net of tax. The building societies have an arrangement with the Inland Revenue whereby it has been agreed that the building society will pay tax at a composite rate, which at the moment is 25 per cent; this is considered the average rate of tax which investors would have paid had they been taxed on income instead of the societies. For the non-tax payer this could, under certain circumstances, be unacceptable as they cannot reclaim the tax deducted.

The names of the accounts at the various building societies differ as the name is a means of marketing and attracting depositors. However, the basic type of account is the share account or ordinary account.

Shares in building societies are not available on the stock market. The share account can be opened by any person, who will then have the right to vote at the general meetings of the building society. They offer a means of depositing funds and when necessary withdrawing funds, without notice and without penalty. The minimum required to open this account is usually £1.

Other forms of accounts offer high interest rates for those who can deposit a large amount of money and leave this on deposit for some considerable time. Often ninety days' notice of withdrawal is required, but should no notice be given then a ninety-day interest penalty is imposed. A most popular type of account is one linked to a cheque service. On this type of account the major building societies will permit the depositor to draw cheques on a bank. That is, the name of the building society is stated as the drawer, but the signature is the name of the building society depositor. On presentation of the cheque to the paying banker, it is debited to the building society's account, and when the cheque is received by the building society, they in turn will debit the account of the depositor. Additionally, customers can obtain funds by using a cash-dispenser card, in the same way as a customer of a bank.

Basically, all building societies will give their accounts attractive names. In principle, the greater the amount deposited and the greater the term, the higher will be the interest earned. The interest credited to the accounts could be paid monthly, quarterly, half-yearly or yearly. A depositor must look closely at the information available.

The other basic service available is that of loans for the purchase of a house. This is often the reason why persons will open an account with a building society. When they have equal to the deposit of a house, they can approach the building society for a loan for the purchase of the property. Usually, a building society will lend up to about 90 per cent of the value of the property, but the loan must not be more than two and a half to three times the gross annual salary of the applicant.

As security, the building society will hold the deeds to the property and expect the mortgagor to insure the property with an insurance company nominated by the building society. Repayment of the mortgage is usually each month and covers both the capital and interest. However, when the interest rate changes, an adjustment may be made in the monthly payments. For example, if interest rates drop, then a lower monthly repayment could be made. (However, should the borrower wish to continue paying at the normal amount, he is likely to repay the debt in a slightly shorter period.) When interest rates rise, the monthly repayment may increase, or alternatively, the time to repay could be extended.

Over a number of years the building societies have been taking away the accounts of individuals from banks. From time to time the banks have reacted to stop this movement, and it seems that in the next few years we shall see even greater competition between the large institutions on both sides of this financial fence.

Some years ago banks only opened their offices from 9.30 am to 3.30 pm and charged their ordinary customers if the balance fell below a minimum or average of about £100. Besides this, tax was payable on interest earned on deposit accounts. Building societies, on the other hand, offered services from 9.30 am to 5 pm and opened Saturday mornings as well. Interest was earned on all sums deposited, which was not only net of tax, but was higher than the gross interest earned in a bank. To counter this, banks have opened some of their offices on a Saturday morning, now offer charge-free accounts provided that the account stays in credit, and as recently as 1985 arranged with the Inland Revenue authorities to pay interest to individuals net of tax.

While banks have expanded their cash-dispenser services, many of the large building societies offer the same type of service. Additionally, building societies now sell traveller's cheques and offer cheque accounts to their customers, as well as standing-order facilities. In this way the ordinary man in the street can obtain the same deposit and withdrawal facilities and at the same time have a pass book in his possession, which gives him immediate reference to his account entries and balance.

In addition to offering charge-free accounts, providing there is a cleared credit balance, banks are also making their borrowing procedures easier and quicker in order to attract more customers.

To take the competition further, the Building Societies Act, which came into force on 1 January 1987, allows building societies to offer the following additional services:

1 Unsecured loans up to £5,000. It is quite likely that the purpose of these loans will be linked to house purchase, but will enable the borrower to use these funds for furniture and house accessories.
2 Provide estate agency and surveying services. One or two banks already own estate agency companies, so that the building societies can offer a complete package to cover the selling, buying, surveying and financing the purchase and sale of property.
3 Offer cheque guarantee cards and overdrafts. This is precisely the same type of service now offered by banks.
4 Offer insurance services. While the insurance subsidiaries of banks will offer a wide range of insurance services to corporate and non corporate customers, this will be limited to non corporate customers and possibly linked to property and contents.
5 Buy and sell shares for customers.
6 Give index-linked or equity mortgage loans.
7 Participate in ownership schemes and help to develop and manage residential land.
8 Own subsidiary companies.
9 Lend in the EEC and other approved countries.

The business of banking

It can be seen, therefore, that the major banks need to ensure that their marketing and services are first class in order to compete with this very important financial sector.

DEPARTMENT OF NATIONAL SAVINGS

This government-owned department works the post offices throughout the UK and offers a variety of securities that are available over the counter or by mail.

National Savings Bank

Originally, this was known as the Post Office Savings Bank, and with 20,000 post offices in the UK it has more branches than any other bank in the country.

The bank offers two types of account, both attracting interest but at different rates. The first account is the ordinary account, which can be opened with as little as £1 but has a maximum of £10,000. The rate of interest will vary from time to time in accordance with the general rate. Currently, the rate is 6 per cent if the balance is over £500, while lower balances will only attract 3 per cent per annum. The first £70 of interest on this account is exempt from income tax. Deposits and withdrawals are recorded in a pass book and the transactions may be made at any post office.

As well as simple deposit and withdrawal facilities, Thomas Cook traveller's cheques can be purchased. Also, standing-order payments can be authorized.

Investment accounts attract a higher rate of interest. As with ordinary accounts the rate of interest will vary from time to time and is calculated on a daily basis. Such interest is not taxed at source and this is clearly a distinct advantage for non-taxpayers. The minimum deposit is £5, while the maximum is £100,000. One month's notice is required for withdrawals.

Unlike the ordinary account which is available to individuals, joint accounts, clubs and societies, investment accounts are also available to corporate bodies.

National Savings Certificates

It is not only the ordinary man in the street who invests his hard-earned savings in this form, but National Savings Certificates are also attractive to the higher-bracket taxpayer. The former invests his money in this form because he knows that it is risk free, earns an attractive rate of interest, it can be put away for five years or more and no further action on his part is necessary and, above all, should there be an urgent need for these funds, then it can be withdrawn with the minimum of fuss. For the higher-level taxpayer, the rate of interest is good, but besides that, at maturity, the return of capital and interest attracts neither capital gains tax nor income tax. For the 60 per cent tax payer, this is very useful.

National Savings Certificates are divided into two distinct groups. The first is the index-linked type, which many years ago were called 'Granny Bonds' and financial columnists still call them this. They are now available to anybody that wishes to purchase them. The minimum purchase is £25 while the maximum is £10,000. No interest is paid, but the value of the certificate is adjusted monthly as from the date of purchase in accordance with the general index of retail prices. With the cost of living, or inflation being low, the government add an additional 4.04 per cent to the current (fourth) issue.

The second group, and the largest, is the ordinary issue, now the thirty-third. Like the index-linked certificates, the minimum purchase is £25 and the maximum is £5,000. They can be held for five years and attract an interest rate of 7.00 per cent. As rates of interest change, so the government is likely to make another issue at a slightly different rate of interest. The higher-level taxpayer, who obtains his interest tax-free, will find it attractive to invest the maximum amount in each issue as they are introduced.

Should any person wish to keep the holdings over the five-year period, then an extension percentage is given. These certificates are not only available to the general public, but also to trustees, friendly societies and charities.

Yearly Plan
A good deal of advertising by the government has gone into bringing this savings scheme to the notice of the general public. This scheme has replaced the old Save As You Earn (SAYE).

This scheme enables a person to make regular savings over a minimum period of one year. On completion of twelve monthly payments a certificate is issued which is held for a further four years. At maturity the capital and interest is repaid with any tax losses. Like the National Savings Certificate, the Yearly Plan Certificate can be held longer and an extension interest rate is given. This rate is publicized in the national press and at post offices.

Income Bonds
These bonds give the investor the opportunity to obtain a regular monthly income. It is particularly useful for those who have retired and been given a lump sum, or for those persons who have been given a redundancy payment. This investment – minimum £2,000 – will begin earning interest from the date of the investment. The interest is paid by the Bonds and Stock Office, on the fifth of each month, either to the holder's bank account or by a crossed warrant sent by post. The interest rate can vary, but six weeks' notice is given in the national press and the post office before any change is made. The interest is paid gross, but must be declared by the beneficiary on his tax return as such income will attract tax.

Deposit Bonds
Should a person not wish to receive his income monthly, then a deposit bond is available which is designed to credit the account annually with the interest earned. Like other forms of national savings, interest rates can be changed from time to time and, again, are advertised when such changes are about to take place. The interest earned on this account is taxable.

Premium Bonds
These bonds, which are issued in units of £1, but the minimum issue is £10, do not attract any interest, but give the holder the opportunity of winning a prize in the weekly and monthly lotteries. To qualify for this lottery the bond must be held for three months. The draw is made by the computer nicknamed ERNIE. The top prize at the moment is £250,000, given monthly, while weekly prizes of £100,000, £50,000 and

£25,000 can be won. Other monthly prizes range from £10,000 down to £50. All prizes are free of income tax.

In order to obtain funds for this lottery, the government will allow the Department of National Savings interest at the rate of 7 per cent on the amount invested. Even with the large number of prizes available, it has been estimated that the chances of winning are 1 in 11,000 for each bond.

Government stocks

Finally, through the National Savings Stock Register, it is possible to buy about fifty government stocks. It is far cheaper to buy stock by this method than through a broker in the Stock Exchange – the commissions are lower, particularly for small amounts. However, the maximum amount that can be invested by an individual is £10,000 any one day.

To purchase a named stock, the order must state the amount of stock the person wishes to buy, or state the amount the person wishes to invest. In both cases the price is quoted in per £100 of nominal stock. The interest earned is paid without deduction of tax, but tax is liable on the income. Such interest can be credited to a National Savings Account, bank account or sent by crossed warrant to the holders address.

PENSION FUNDS

Very often this form of saving may be the only form of saving that an individual may make. It is the remuneration that a person is entitled to when he has finished active work.

There are various kinds of pension schemes. For example, a large number of bank clerks make no contribution to a pension fund yet on retirement will receive up to one-sixtieth of the salary for each year of employment. Others, for example teachers, will make a contribution of 6 per cent of their salary in order to have a pension of one-eightieth of their salary for each year in employment.

For the self-employed, a contribution from profits is made to a pension fund which is contracted with an insurance company or some other financial institution. This annual contribution will provide a lump sum and a pension on retirement. Often an insurance endowment policy is chosen as an alternative.

The employee who has not got the benefit of a pension scheme with his employer, will be contracted into the government scheme and payment is made by deduction of an amount through the weekly or monthly wage packet.

In all cases there is either a voluntary or compulsory form of savings which obviously reduces the amount of money that would otherwise be in a bank account.

INSURANCE SCHEMES

Although one talks of 'insurance', this word refers to inanimate objects – that is a house can be insured, its contents, or a car can be insured. Thus should a loss occur, a payment by the insurance company will be made. Should there be no accident and therefore no loss, the owner will pay premiums without any return.

For life, then, a premium is paid for an assurance policy. That is a payment will eventually be made, either on reaching a certain age or upon death. Life assurance has three basic characteristics: (1) it is essentially long term, (2) it deals with an event that will eventually happen and (3) an annual premium is agreed and is paid either monthly, quarterly, half-yearly or yearly. There are various policies available to an individual.

Whole-life policies
This form of policy will yield a lump sum at death. It is therefore only the heirs or beneficiaries that benefit from a policy of this nature. As no value can be placed on a persons life, nor does anyone know when they will die, the insurance companies will from their statistics calculate a premium and the relative payment that can be paid at death.

Endowment policies
This policy will offer a lump sum at a certain age, often between sixty and sixty-five, or a payment will be made upon death, whichever is the sooner. The attraction of this form of policy is that when a person reaches an age when he either no

longer wishes to work or is unable to work, a lump sum is at his disposal.

An endowment policy can be provided either 'with profits' or 'without profits'. A with-profits policy can be obtained for an extra premium, and the policy-holder will share in the fortunes of the company and is entitled to some of the profits which are declared as bonuses – often each year. These bonuses are usually paid out at maturity of the policy. The without-profits policy involves slightly lower premiums, attracting some interest, but no bonuses are payable at maturity.

Term policies
This type of policy is one which covers an individual for a particular period. These may be taken out for a few weeks – for a holiday – or for a number of years. Should the person die within the period of the policy, then the beneficiaries will obtain some benefit. Should the person survive that period, then there is no benefit.

Annuities
This is particularly attractive to the older person who wishes to contribute a lump sum to an assurance company. At an agreed date an income is paid for the rest of the life of the individual Obviously, the longer the money is left with the company before withdrawal, the larger the annual income. So far as the company is concerned, a person who lives a long life will make a good profit, but against that, those who die early will fail to make a profit.

Life policies in general represent a genuine saving as it gives financial protection to dependants; additionally, it provides a person with a lump sum on retirement and can be used to supplement a pension. A bank will look very favourably on a borrower who has made provision to pay a regular premium for an endowment policy. It assures the bank that the customer has a savings disposition early in his or her life and that repayment of the loan is more likely to be repaid.

SHARES

It is a well known fact that the majority of shares are held by institutions such as trade unions, pensions funds and insurance companies, but with government encouragement share ownership is becoming more widespread, particularly with the privatization of British Telecom, British Gas, TSB England and Wales, and so on. It is also noticed that many companies are issuing shares to employees and customers.

People buy shares for different reasons. Some buy them for a possible quick profit, particulary when there is a rumour of a takeover, new invention, mineral find or perhaps the anticipation of higher than average profits. However, the majority of investors will take a long view and invest funds in select companies who they think are strong and will expand, thereby offering increased dividends over a long period. At the same time the value of the share will increase at least at the rate of inflation.

Stockbrokers will assist investors by advising them not only on the state of the company, but also of the industry and the stock market as a whole. They will inform the investor whether they consider the shares to be cheap or dear and make recommendations based on the research that they do as part of their overall activity. Other persons will base the decisions to buy or sell on their ability to predict particular patterns in the market. They may be right or wrong.

The risks involved in buying shares should not be underestimated. Even large well-known companies have been known to have sharp reversals and reduced profits. Those involved in giving advice to the public on investment always suggest that this form of investment should not be undertaken by those for whom a loss of money will cause undue hardship.

STOCKS

The safest type of investment is the purchase of government securities. These are known as gilt-edged. Stocks are unlike shares in that they do not represent an investment in a company (i.e. part of the capital) but are a loan to the government or local authority.

There are well over a hundred government stocks in existence as well as stock issued by local authorities. These stocks are issued in amounts of £100. The purchase price can be either higher or lower than this par value, but the interest quoted is based on £100 stock. As these are loans, the stock will in the vast majority of cases indicate the date of repayment. The price of stock will be representative of current interest rates. If interest rates fall, stock will be more attractive to buy and its price will therefore rise. Of course the reverse is also true. When interest rates rise, the price of stock will tend to fall.

Other than government and local government stock offering fixed interest, there are a few stocks which do not offer any interest at all, but are index-linked, so that the repayment value is dependent on the Retail Price Index.

Less secure, are the stocks offered by companies. These are also loans, but in order to make them attractive, slightly higher rate of interest is offered and they are usually secured, or debentured. Some corporate stock are issued without security to the investor.

With such a wide range of stocks available, it is possible for the investor to choose one which is either short term or long term; one which is for capital growth or for income. Government stocks which yield a capital gain are exempt from capital gains tax.

INVESTMENT TRUSTS

These types of company raise funds from the public in order to invest in other companies. Their stock in trade are the shares and stocks held. For the small investor, it gives him or her the opportunity to spread the risk of investment over a wide range of securities controlled by a full-time investment specialist.

Investment trust companies are merely limited companies registered under the Companies Act. Their capital is raised from the public, either in the form of ordinary shares, preference shares or debentures. With these funds, they invest in the capital of other companies. The management of an investment trust will take decisions on buying and selling any security, and by receiving dividends and profits on buying and selling they will be able to give their shareholders dividends and increase the value of the shares in their company.

With no exchange control regulations in this country, many investment trust companies have found it attractive and profitable to invest their funds abroad, particularly Japan. They provide a very attractive form of investment to those who have limited funds and wish to spread investment risks.

UNIT TRUSTS

A unit trust is a form of investment whereby the funds of many investors are placed into a financial pool. This total amount of money is invested by the trust management into securities on behalf of the investors. The advantages of a units trust is the security, regular income and/or capital appreciation and the spread of risk.

The portfolio of securities is the unit and this is divided into thousands of sub-units which are sold to the public. The investor will buy a specified number of units and will be given a certificate to represent his holding. The value of the unit will fluctuate and the market price will depend upon the investment expertise of the management. The dividends from the investments are received by the management and profits made by the purchase of sale of shares are distributed to the unit trust holders, less expenses twice each year. Each shareholder will be paid in proportion to his holding. Many unit trusts exist for capital growth only and consequently reinvest all dividends received and issue no dividends to the unit holders. Over a period of time the value of the units should increase.

The investor is able to purchase and sell his units direct to the company. There is no need to act through a bank or stockbroker. Many unit trusts have the facility to enable the investor to either buy or sell by telephone, confirming the deal by a written contract within a day or two.

Looking at any national newspaper it is possible to see unit trust companies offering a variety of unit trusts. Most specialize in some form or other, for example smaller companies, Europe, gilts, income, minerals.

The investment in any unit trust is usually a minimum of £500, but in order to attract investments, many give the small investor the opportunity to invest a regular amount each month, usually a minimum of £25. This latter method is particularly attractive to persons who wish to be involved in some form of investment but have not got a large sum immediately available. It enables the person to see a build up of savings with possible capital growth.

PERSONAL EQUITY PLAN

This plan, known as PEP, was introduced in the 1986 Budget. It gives the small investor the opportunity of investing a regular amount each month, up to a limit of £2,400 per annum, into securities quoted on the Stock Exchange. These PEPs will be arranged by unit trusts, investment trusts and banks who are involved in portfolio management.

The investor will be given some choice of the type of security he would like to place his funds in, and providing he holds these investments for a specified time, no capital gains tax is payable on any profits made.

MISCELLANEOUS INVESTMENTS

There are very many people who do not invest their surplus cash in either bank deposit accounts, stocks and shares, or National Savings Certificates, and so on. They combine a hobby with investment and buy all kinds of collectable things, such as paintings, stamps or china. However, there is often a conflict between the collection for pleasure and the pursuit of wealth.

These collection have obvious drawbacks. In themselves they provide no income; moreover, whatever the collection, expense is involved in providing such things as insurance and accommodation. Needless to say, the value of any item is subject to market fluctuations, and when a person need funds he may find that there is no market or that the price has been considerably reduced. Nevertheless, the various advertisements of auctions that can be seen in national newspapers for objects d'art indicates the interest shown in this type of investment.

For any person entering this market, extreme caution must be exercised as it is the easiest thing in the world to spend money on some object which you consider has a scarcity value or is genuine, only to find that it has neither. However, for most people, collecting is as much a pleasure as a hedge against inflation.

Competition for loans to individuals

Having dealt with the competitors of banks for deposits, there are many types of institutions that compete with banks to lend money to various borrowers. As we have said, building societies at the moment compete with banks in lending money for house purchase and house improvement. Shortly, they will compete in lending money for other domestic purposes.

CREDIT CARD COMPANIES

Credit card companies, though wholly owned by banks, are independent separate companies and encourage card-holders to borrow money from them. It is true that the interest rates charged are greater than those available from banks on overdrafts and loans, nevertheless a lot of people maintain large loans from credit card companies. Often such loans are high risk with considerable losses to the companies concerned.

PRIVATE LOANS

We shall never really know how much money is loaned by one person to another. This may be a parent lending a son or daughter some money to buy a suit of clothes for an interview for his or her first job. The loans could be to pay for enrolment fees and textbooks to study for a professional diploma. It could be for a car or, indeed, any other need. This is perhaps the most common form of lending/borrowing.

Often it involves no payment of interest, no deposit of security and the lender is only too pleased to lend for a good purpose.

Other forms of loans could be for business purposes. This will involve some written evidence of the debt, payment of interest and repayment of the debt by a given date.

Whatever the reason for private borrowing, it does save the embarrassment of going to a complete stranger to give a reason for borrowing, discussing intimate personal details and then at the end of it either receiving a refusal or a loan with stringent conditions.

CREDIT UNIONS

A credit union is based on people with a common interest. They may either work together or live in the same buildings or flats. It may take the form of a social club with an additional interest in members investing their funds into a pool which gives the investors a given rate of interest. These funds are placed in a safe or relatively risk-free investment or could be used to lend to other members a stated sum of money either to help them over a difficult time or for the purchase of some domestic commodity. In this way the members of the community help each other.

The lending decision is made by an elected committee, not necessarily experienced in giving loans, but who take into consideration the various factors before a decision is made.

These unions are extremely useful as their members tend to be on low income, often with no bank account, and would by necessity be driven into the arms of loan sharks, who would charge them an extremely high interest rate, and they would find themselves getting deeper and deeper into debt.

Credit unions are extremely popular in the USA and are recognized and controlled by state legislation. In this country it is the West Indian community that predominate in this area. There are over seventy unions in this country, each with up to 1,000 members.

The Credit Union Act 1979 provides for the registration of a society and defines the objects of a union (promoting thrift, creating sources of credit, training and education of its

INSURANCE COMPANIES

Although insurance companies have already been discussed in this chapter as organizations that take regular deposits from individuals in the form of premiums on various forms of assurance, they are also lenders of money, and often a person would find it easier and often cheaper to approach an insurance company with whom he has an assurance contract, to lend him funds against the security of the policy. The amount the insurance company is willing to lend often depends on the surrender value of the policy or policies. Providing the reason for borrowing is reasonable, the society would have no hesitation in granting an advance.

FINANCE HOUSES

These institutions were at their peak some twenty years or so, just after Second World War, when there was a shortage of funds, due to strict government control of credit. When buying on credit, government regulations laid down the minimum deposit that had to be given, the maximum length of time permitted for the loan, the rate of interest to be paid and other factors. The finance houses, many of them now owned by banks, offer hire purchase, credit instalment business and leasing facilities.

The funds for these companies come from three main sources: first, from the banks, from whom they obtain loans and deposits; Second, from trading in discounted bills; third, from deposits from the public.

The finance houses will take deposits from large and small banks and hold these funds, very often for short periods. The reason is that when banks have surplus funds, they will invest elsewhere and obtain whatever interest they can attract. The finance houses are quite willing to take these funds and utilize them for their own purposes. Since funds are moving each day, they do of course keep careful control of the situation.

Should the finance house need funds, it can draw a bill of exchange on a bank, which it presents to the bank for acceptance and can then offer it to the money market, thereby obtaining ready funds at the face value of the bill less any interest charges demanded by the purchaser of the bill. In this way the finance house can obtain funds for three or six months or, if necessary, even longer.

Perhaps the most important source of funds are those the company obtains by advertising for deposits from the public at large. Often the minimum sum is about £1,000 and is deposited for a fixed period of up to one year, occasionally two years. Larger deposits (e.g. public companies) will also deposit surplus funds with them since the interest rates offered are usually very attractive in comparison with other financial institutions. The funds so generated will be used to offer hire purchase facilities, credit sales agreements and leasing services.

A hire purchase agreement, as the name suggests, is a contract of hire, and payment for the goods is made by regular instalments. The article does not become the property of the hirer until the last instalment has been paid.

A credit sales agreement, often called instalment trading, is one where the ownership is immediately transferred to the purchaser, even though payment will be made by instalments and final settlement will not be made for twelve or twenty-four months. In the case of leasing, the company will request the finance house to purchase an asset, e.g. property, a fleet of cars, a computer, etc. This asset is then leased to the company by the finance house for a stated number of years for a given amount. This form of contract is attractive both to the lessor and lessee. The lessor, the finance house, obtains a considerable tax allowance on purchase, while the lessee does not spend needy capital but pays an annual sum which is considered as an expense to the business and thereby attracts a tax allowance. Although in recent years the tax allowances have been reduced, this is still a very attractive way of utilizing assets.

MISCELLANEOUS METHODS OF BORROWING

Pawn shops and money lenders

Other forms of competition for banks are the pawn shops and loan companies that are often seen in both small towns and cities. Pawn shops and loan companies still have a function in this country even though there are a wide range of financial institutions only too willing to lend money. This applies especially to banks, who through advertising, particularly on television, are giving the indication that not only are they only too willing to give a quick answer to a lending proposition but they are also willing to say yes.

Pawn shops usually operate in the poorer districts of a town, and loan companies advertise through journals, local newspapers, etc. In both cases, the interest rates are usually very much higher than bank lending rates or credit instalment rates. One often hears stories of a person who has got himself or herself in the clutches of a money lender and because of the rate of interest imposed, is unable to free himself of the debt.

It seems that there are people who feel unable to enter a bank and discuss their problems with an official, because they find a bank building too intimidating or the atmosphere unwelcoming. Instead they prefer the pawn shop at the bottom of the road where an article of some value is given as security against a loan, or the informality of a money-lender even though they know the cost of borrowing in both cases will be much higher.

Money shops

Despite the fact that the major banks are opening Saturday morning, offering cash-dispensing facilities, money shops, usually financed by the large American banks, are opening offices in various streets. They offer a less formal attitude to their customers, they are bright, comfortable places and are designed to attract the individual. In the main they offer lending services, but are also willing to take deposits, offering deposit and savings accounts that will provide various rates of interest. For those persons who wish to have deposit and withdrawal services, earn some interest on their accounts, yet find the 'shop' open from 9 am to 5 pm each working day, six days a week, they offer a good service.

These money shops in recent years have expanded, building up a good customer base, but like the pawnbrokers and loan companies, they tend to lend money to those who would be considered poor credit risks; consequently, they do have an exposure to bad debts, so the interest rates charged are inevitably higher than those charged by the banks.

Conclusion

It seems that banks face tremendous competition for deposits and loans. Yet each year the major clearing banks report increased profits and often an increase in the numbers of customers on their books. How is this possible?

First, the banks themselves are trying to reduce the formidable image they once gave to the ordinary man in the street. We have had advertisements showing the 'bank manager in the cupboard', 'the action bank' 'the bank that says Yes', 'the listening bank', and so on. All these advertisements are trying to give banks a human face.

Reinforcing these major advertising campaigns is the fact that they are making the various branches less formidable places to enter: the staff in many banks are in front of the counter and easily available to the customer for consultation. Unlike in the 1940s, bank managers will go out to factories, industrial estates, housing estates and 'sell' their bank, rather than sitting in their office waiting for customers to come to them. School children and young college students can be given talks by members of banks or the Banking Information Service on the various services of banks and the ways they can help the individual. Education is also playing its part in ensuring that in its business, commercial, secretarial and life-skill courses, knowledge of banking is taught.

Despite all this competition, banks are facing reality by reducing the cost of maintaining an account with them to zero – if the customer is in credit. There is no cost in obtaining a cheque book, a paying-in book and regular statements as frequently as required.

Additionally, customers may open various types of deposit

accounts which will attract interest on a daily basis at current rates, and by having an account with the bank various other services are also available, for example standing orders, direct debits, foreign currency and traveller's cheques. Many of these services are not available at other financial institutions.

It must also be recognized that with progress in the field of information technology, it will be possible to contact the bank via a home computer and receive information, transfer money and do many other functions from home. The credit card services that allows customers to purchase goods and services will probably expand while the availability of cash from cash-dispensers will continue to grow and the increasing interchangeability of cards between one bank and another will continue. We now have the use of cash-dispenser cards between National Westminster Bank, Midland Bank and TSB. It is this variety of services that will continue to attract the corporate and non-corporate customer.

To these facts must be added the lethargy of the individual. It is said that once a person opens an account with a bank, it is more than likely that person will stay with the bank for the rest of his or her life. Whether this will continue will depend on many things. Customers become dependent on banks to receive their salaries, dividend payments and various sundry receipts. They also become dependent on banks in making their regular payments for mortgages, rates, insurance and other expenses. Finally, there is a certain satisfaction that banks can offer, either directly or through their subsidiaries, all the possible financial services that are likely to be required. All that is required is a visit or telephone call to the local branch.

Self-examination questions

1. Describe the difference between a Treasury bill and a certificate of deposit.
2. A public limited company can, if necessary, obtain funds by means of a 'rights issue'. Describe the procedure involved for this event to take place.
3. Compare the services that are offered to an individual by a building society with those offered by a clearing bank.
4. Describe some of the steps that have been taken by banks, to counter the competition of the building societies.
5. List the services offered by the National Savings Department. How many of these are available through a bank?
6. What is the difference between 'insurance' and 'assurance'?
7. What is the difference between a stock and a share?
8. State the advantages of investing in a unit trust for the small investor.
9. What are the disadvantages of investing funds in objects d'art.
10. Describe at least four services available from a bank that are not available from any other financial institution.

Appendices

The law relating to banking springs mainly from two sources: the law as laid down by Parliament (Acts, statutes) and judgments made in the civil courts (known as case law or precedents). Appendices I and II offer some case-note facts and the judgment at the court, as well as providing brief extracts from the principal statutes affecting bankers. Appendix III contains specimen examination questions from the first examination paper set on the subject, in May 1987, by the Chartered Institute of Bankers.

Appendix I: Relevant case law

The following cases are presented in alphabetical order.

Baines v. National Provincial Bank Ltd (1927)

A transaction was completed some five minutes after the bank's normal closing time. However, the customer had been present on the premises prior to closing time and it was held that this transaction was a payment within the ordinary course of business.

Bevan v. National Bank Ltd (1906)

The bank enquired as to why a cheque made payable to a company and crossed 'account payee' was being paid into a personal account. They were told that the individual was trading in the company name. This was not true – the individual was in fact employed by the company. The bank, however, was not held by the court to be negligent, because they had made an enquiry.

Box v. Midland Bank Ltd (1979)

A bank manager mistakenly gave a customer the impression that a loan would be granted to him. The manager failed to make it clear that the ultimate decision did not lie with him. The customer went ahead and acted on the assumption that the loan would be forthcoming. He entered into a contract which he could not pay for without the loan. He sued the bank for negligence.

Held: The bank manager was under a duty to take reasonable care when giving advice regarding a loan. He was careless in leaving the customer with the impression that the loan would be granted, therefore the bank was liable in negligence.

Brown v. Westminster Bank Ltd (1964)

The lady plaintiff had reassured the bank that her signature as a drawer on a cheque was genuine, since on various occasions, the manager had made enquiries. It turned out that about a hundred of her cheques carried a forged drawer's signature.

Held: since she had authorized some signatures and failed to inform the bank that a series of forgeries had taken place, the bank had acted correctly in debiting her account. She had breached her duty to take care.

Burnett v. Westminster Bank Ltd (1966)

Mr Burnett had accounts at both Borough and Bromley branches. Using a Borough cheque, he altered the branch name to draw a cheque payable at Bromley. He then stopped the cheque; but the cheque was processed on its magnetic ink without the alteration being noted.

Held: the bank were liable as it paid out on a cheque which had been countermanded.

Coutts & Co. v. Browne-Lecky (1947)

The bank lent money to a minor. He failed to repay the money. The bank tried to enforce the guarantee, but as this was linked to a transaction that itself was not legally enforcible, the bank did not succeed. (Loans to a minor are void under the Infants Relief Act 1874.)

Davidson v. Barclays Bank Ltd (1940)

The bank mistakenly paid out on a stopped cheque. This left the plaintiff's account with no funds in it, so a subsequent cheque was returned marked 'not sufficient'. It was held by the courts that these words, given that the cheque was wrongfully dishonoured, were libellous. The bank were required to pay £250 in compensation to Mr Davidson.

Foley v. Hill (1848)

This case established that the banker is not under an obligation to inform the customer about the use made of the money, since the banker is not a trustee as such. The banker is a debtor for the amount borrowed.

Greenwood v. Martins Bank Ltd (1933)

Mrs Greenwood took to drawing money out of her husband's account by forging her husband's signature. Mr Greenwood found out about the forgeries but did nothing about them until after his wife's death. He then made a claim against the bank in conversion.

Held: The bank was entitled to debit Mr Greenwood's account since he had breached the customer's duty not to facilitate forgery.

Hedley Byrne & Co. Ltd v. Heller & Partners (1966)

The defendant bank gave a reference concerning the credit rating of a third party. The reference proved inaccurate as the subject went into liquidation. Hedley Byrne had lent a large sum of money on the strength of the status report. They sued in negligence.

Held: The merchant bank did owe a duty of care to the person relying on the credit reference. Moreover, they were negligent in giving that statement but they did not have to pay compensation because they had headed the report, 'without responsibilty'.

House Property Company of London Ltd v. London, County & Westminster Bank (1915)

A cheque (crossed 'account payee') was made payable to a named person and 'others or bearer'. A bearer paid the cheque into his own account. It transpired that the bearer wasn't entitled to the cheque or the proceeds. The true owners sued the bank.

Held: The court took the view that where a cheque is

crossed 'account payee', to pay that cheque into an account for someone other than a specified payee and without enquiry would be negligence on the part of the bank.

Joachimson v. Swiss Bank Corporation (1921)

This case laid down the duties of each of the two parties in the contractual arrangement as described in the main text. In addition, it was stated that the relationship between the two parties could be described as that of debtor and creditor and that the onus was on the creditor (i.e. the customer) to seek out the money owed by the debtor (the bank) – thus reversing the normal rules.

King's North Trust Ltd v. Bell and others (1985)

The husband was the sole legal owner of the matrimonial home, but his wife, Mrs Bell, had acquired an equitable interest by contributing to the purchase price. The mortgagors required both parties to sign the mortgage deed. The husband's solicitors were meant to arrange this. In practice, Mr Bell had taken the mortgage deed home and had obtain Mrs Bell's signature. The mortgagor's tried to repossess in event of default. Mrs Bell said she should not be bound by the deed.

Held: The Court of Appeal agreed with Mrs Bell. She could remain in possession. The mortgagors ought to have insisted that Mrs Bell received independent financial advice.

Ladbroke & Co. v. Todd (1914)

A rogue who stole a cheque (which was crossed 'account payee') opened an account with the stolen cheque at the defendant bank. Once the cheque was cleared, the rogue withdrew all the money and disappeared. It was held that the bank had been negligent in their failure to take a reference. The bank had to repay the true owner the proceeds.

Langtry v. Union Bank of London (1896)

The actress Lily Langtry sued the defendant bank, who handed over her jewellery to a thief. The thief had forged Miss Langtry's signature. The case was settled by giving Miss Langtry compensation prior to the court case being heard.

Lloyds Bank Ltd v. Brooks (1950)

Lady Brooks was credited with income from shares that she did not possess. The bank had made a mistake on the statement. The plaintiff, meanwhile, relying on the bank's information as to her position, had spent the money. It was held that the bank was not entitled to claim the money back since the plaintiff had already honestly acted on the wrong information.

Lloyds Bank Ltd v. Bundy (1975)

Mr Bundy was an elderly farmer. His son, the company his son was involved in and the elderly farmer all used the same branch of Lloyds. The son's company's overdraft (some £1,500) was guaranteed by old Mr Bundy. His only asset was the farmhouse in which he lived. Further increases on overdraft, backed by guarantee, followed. A representative from Lloyds called at the farm and told Mr Bundy senior that unless he was willing to make fresh guarantees (now standing at £11,000) his son's company would no longer benefit from the bank's overdraft. Mr Bundy complied with this pressure. The son's company went into liquidation and the bank wanted to possess the farmhouse.

Held: The Court of Appeal held that the bank could not enforce the guarantee on the grounds of 'undue influence'. Mr Bundy senior had been reliant solely on the bank for advice on his financial affairs. The bank's interest in having the guarantee signed meant that the bank could not give impartial advice. Also, they failed to insist that Mr Bundy receive impartial advice from another source. They had breached the special relationship that existed between the two parties.

London Joint Stock Bank Ltd v. MacMillan & Arthur (1918)

The partner defendants in this case obligingly signed a cheque made out by their clerk for £20. However, the cheque omitted to state the amount in words. The clerk fraudulently altered the amount to £120, writing in the appropriate words. He cashed the cheque. The partners claimed conversion from the bank.

Held: The bank was entitled to make the debit on the partnership account because the partnership as a customer had failed to take reasonable care and had breached its contractual duty not to facilitate fraud.

Moynihan v. National Bank Ltd (1969)

An out-of-court settlement pertained in this case. The plaintiff alleged that the bank had acted negligently and this had resulted in a loss of jewellery from a bank raid. Both parties reached a private settlement. (Banks should advise their customers to obtain appropriate insurance cover for deposited goods.)

National Westminster Bank PLC v. Morgan (1985)

A married couple were co-legal owners of their home and the bank had obtained Mrs Morgan's signature on their mortgage deed. The bank manager had called at the house for the signature and she had signed in the knowledge that if the bank did not make the loan, the house would be lost to other creditors. When her husband died, she asked the court to release her from the obligation on the grounds of undue influence.

Held: The House of Lords found in the bank's favour, finding no undue influence on Mrs Morgan to create the deed.

Prosperity Ltd v. Lloyds Bank Ltd (1923)

This case confirmed that a bank has a duty to give reasonable notice to close an account. What is 'reasonable notice' will depend on the circumstances. A month's notice was not enough where the account was that of a company for whom closure led to widespread ramifications.

R. v. Andover Justices ex p. Rhodes (1980)

A husband was a customer of a bank. His wife was accused of theft and she claimed that the proceeds of the crime had been paid into her husband's bank account. The police obtained a court order under the Bankers' Books Evidence Act 1879 to inspect the husband's account. The husband challenged the order.

Held: The evidence sought was necessary and relevant to the crime charged. There were no grounds for refusing the order and disclosure.

Tournier v. National Provincial and Union Bank of England (1924)

There is a duty on behalf of the bank to maintain secrecy, this case determined, but there are instances where this confidence may be breached without the customer's consent. Such exceptional circumstances might be where it is in the bank's interest to do so; where it is in the interest of the public to do so and where required by law. Also, it may be possible to imply consent from certain actions, such as where a husband allows his wife to collect statements on his behalf.

United Dominions Trust v. Kirkwood (1966)

This case held that the UDT were a bank. An organization that fell within the definition of a bank was one which:
1 Accepted money from customers
2 Collected money on behalf of customers
3 Honoured cheques drawn by customers.

A. L. Underwood Ltd v. Bank of Liverpool and Martins Ltd (1924)

Over a long period of time the bank credited a personal account (that of the managing director) with cheques made payable to a company. The court ruled that the bank had committed conversion with the company's money. The bank were negligent in not making an enquiry.

Whitehead v. National Westminster Bank Ltd (1982)

The customer had signed a standing-order mandate. On the date due for payment insufficient funds were available and the bank failed to honour the mandate. The customer claimed that the bank should have continued to check the account because sufficient funds were eventually deposited.

Held: The bank were under no obligation to keep checking. A standing-order mandate need only be honoured if adequate funds are in the account on the due date.

Williams & Glyn's Bank Ltd v. Barnes (1980)

The defendant director had borrowed a lot of money from the bank in order to buy shares in a company, which later went into liquidation. The company was one to which the bank had given overdraft facilities. Mr Barnes claimed he did not have to pay the money back because the bank had been negligent in not advising him against the borrowing.

Held: The bank were not negligent; they had done precisely what was asked – the customer made no specific request for advice on whether the borrowing was sound.

Mr Barnes also claimed that he did not have to repay the amount borrowed because the bank had no right to demand immediate repayment of an overdraft. The court said that an overdraft is repayable on demand where there is no agreed date for repayment or no terms which imply that reasonable notice is required. A phrase such as 'on the usual banking conditions' would not by itself rule out the possibility of reasonable notice.

Williams & Glyn's Bank Ltd v. Boland and another (1980)

The husband and wife in this case bought a house with their joint earnings, but the house was registered as being the property of the husband. Later the husband offered the home as security for a loan without telling his wife. The husband then failed to keep up the repayments and the bank sought to possess the house.

Held: The House of Lords confirmed the Court of Appeal's view that the wife, as an occupier that had contributed to the costs of the home, had an overriding interest. This interest entitled the wife to remain in possession, in the face of the bank's claim.

Williams & Glyn's Bank Ltd v. Brown (1980)

Arrived at the same decision as the Boland case.

Woods v. Martins Bank Ltd (1959)

The bank manager had advised Mr Woods to invest in a company which had an account at the same branch. The investment turned out badly but the bank was liable not because of this but because the manager had not met the standard of care a customer could expect from a banker.

Held: The case confirmed that the banker and customer relationship came into being when the bank took responsibility for this aspect of the customer's affairs.

Appendix II: Important statutes

The following Acts are presented in alphabetical order.

Bankers' Books Evidence Act 1879 (s.7)

On the the application of any party to a legal proceeding a court or judge may order that such party be at liberty to inspect and take copies of entries in a bankers book for any of the purposes of such proceedings. [*Note*: Under the Banking Act 1979, schedule 6, paragraph 1, this power to compel inspection under Section 7 extends to entries recorded on microfilm.]

Banking Act 1979: controlling deposit-taking

S.1 Except as provided by Section 2 below, no person may accept a deposit in the course of carrying on a business which is a deposit taking business for the purpose of this Act. . . . A business is a deposit taking business for the purpose of this Act if . . .

(a) in the course of the business money received by way of deposit is lent to others or
(b) any other activity of the business is financed, wholly or to any material extent, out of the capital of or the interest on money received by way of deposit.

S.3 RECOGNITION AND LICENSING OF A BANK

(1) Recognition as a bank for the purposes of this Act may be granted by the Bank on an application in that behalf by the institution concerned . . .

. . .

(3) (a) The Bank shall not grant to an institution recognition as a bank unless it is satisfied that the criteria in Part 1 of Schedule 2 to this Act are fulfilled with respect to the institution and

(b) The Bank shall not grant a full licence to an institution unless it is satisfied that the criteria in Part II of that Schedule are fulfilled with respect to the institution.
(4) The Bank shall grant neither recognition or a licence to an institution which is not a body corporate if the whole of the assets are available to the institution are owned by a single individual.

SCHEDULE 2, PART I MINIMUM CRITERIA FOR DEPOSIT-TAKING INSTITUTIONS

The institution enjoys, and has for a reasonable period of time enjoyed, a high reputation and standing in the financial community . . .

. . .

2(2) An institution shall not be regarded as providing a wide range of banking services at any time unless . . . it provides at that time all of the following services namely
   (a) current or deposit account facilities in sterling or foreign currency for members of the public or for bodies corporate or the acceptance of funds in sterling or foreign currency in the wholesale money markets;
   (b) finance in the form of overdraft or loan facilities in sterling or foreign currency for members of the public or for bodies corporate or the lending of funds in sterling or foreign currency in the wholesale money markets.
   (c) foreign exchange services for domestic and foreign customers
   (d) finance through the medium of bills of exchange and promissory notes together with finance for foreign trade and documentation in connection with foreign trade; and
   (e) financial advice for members of the public and for bodies corporate or investment management services and facilities for arranging the purchase and sale of securities in sterling or foreign currencies.

. . .

2(5) . . . the institution will at the time recognition is granted have net assets which amount to not less than:
  (a) £5 million, if it is an institution which provides or will provide a wide range of banking services; and
  (b) £250,000, if it provides or will provide a highly specialised banking service.

Bills of Exchange Act 1882

S.3 DEFINES A BILL OF EXCHANGE

(1) An unconditional order in writing, addressed by one person to another, signed by the person giving it, requiring the person to whom it is addressed to pay on demand or at a fixed or determinable future time a sum certain in money to or to the order of a specified person, or to bearer.
(2) An instrument which does not comply with these conditions, or which orders any act to be done in addition to the payment of money, is not a bill of exchange.
(3) An order to pay out of a particular fund is not unconditional within the meaning of this section; but an unqualified order to pay, coupled with (a) an indication of a particular fund out of which the drawee is to reimburse himself or a particular account to be debited with the amount, or (b) a statement of the transaction which gives rise to the bill, is unconditional.

  A bill is not valid by reason:
  (a) That it is not dated;
  (b) That it does not comply with the value given, or that any value has been given therefor;
  (c) That it does not specify the place where it is drawn or the place where it is payable.

S.29 DEFINES A HOLDER IN DUE COURSE

(1) A holder in due course is a holder who has taken a bill, complete and regular on the face of it, under the following conditions; namely,

(a) That he became the holder of it before it was overdue, and without notice that it had been previously dishonoured, if such was the fact;
(b) That he took the bill in good faith and for value, and that the time the bill was negotiated to him he had no notice of any defect in the title of the person who negotiated it.

(2) In particular, the title of a person who negotiates a bill is defective within the meaning of this Act when he obtained the bill or the acceptance thereof, by fraud, duress or force and fear, or other unlawful means, or for an illegal consideration or when he negotiates it in breach of faith, or under circumstances as amount to a fraud.

(3) A holder (whether for value or not), who derives his title to a bill through a holder in due course, and who is not himself a party to any fraud or illegality affecting it, has all the rights of that holder in due course as regards the acceptor and all parties to the bill prior to that holder.

S.31 NEGOTIATING BILLS

(1) A bill is negotiated when it is transferred from one person to another in such a manner as to constitute the transferee the holder of the bill.
(2) A bill payable to bearer is negotiated by delivery.
(3) A bill payable to order is negotiated by the indorsement of the holder completed by delivery.
(4) Where the holder of a bill payable to his order transfers it for value without indorsing it, the transfer gives the transferee such title as the transferor had in the bill, and the transferee in addition acquires the right to have the indorsement of the transferor.
(5) Where any person is under obligation to indorse a bill in a representative capacity, he may indorse the bill in such terms as to negative personal liability.

S.34 INDORSEMENT IN BLANK AND SPECIAL INDORSEMENT

(1) An indorsement in blank specifies no indorsee, and a bill so indorsed becomes payable to bearer.

(2) A special indorsement specifies the person to whom, or to whose order, the bill is to be payable.
(3) The provisions of this Act relating to a payee apply with the necessary modifications to an indorsee under a special indorsement.
(4) When a bill has been indorsed in blank, any holder may convert the blank indorsement into a special indorsement by writing above the indorser's signature a direction to pay the bill to or to the order of himself or some other person.

S.38 RIGHTS OF THE HOLDER

The rights and powers of the holder of a bill are as follows:

(1) He may sue on the bill in his own name;
(2) Where he is a holder in due course, he holds the bill free from any defect of title of prior parties, as well as from mere personal defences available to prior parties among themselves, and may enforce payment against all parties liable on the bill;
(3) Where his title is defective (a) if he negotiates the bill to a holder in due course, that holder obtains a good and complete title to the bill, and (b) if he obtains payment of the bill the person who pays him in due course gets a valid discharge for the bill.

S.73 DEFINITION OF A CHEQUE

A cheque is a bill of exchange drawn on a banker payable on demand.

Except as otherwise provided in this Part, the provisions of this Act applicable to a bill of exchange payable on demand apply to a cheque.

S.75 REVOCATION OF BANKER'S AUTHORITY

The duty and authority of a banker to pay a cheque drawn on him by his customer are determined by:

(1) Countermand of payment;
(2) Notice of the customer's death.

S.76 GENERAL AND SPECIAL CROSSINGS ON A CHEQUE

(1) Where a cheque bears across its face an addition of:
   (a) The words 'and company' or any abbreviation thereof between two parallel transverse lines, either with or without the words 'not negotiable'; or;
   (b) Two parallel transverse lines simply, either with or without the words 'not negotiable';
   that addition constitutes a crossing, and the cheque is crossed generally.
(2) Where a cheque bears across its face an addition of the name of a banker, either with or without the words 'not negotiable', that addition constitutes a crossing, and the cheque is crossed specially and to that banker.

S.79 THE DUTIES OF A BANKER AND THE CROSSED CHEQUE

(1) Where a cheque is crossed specially to more than one banker, except when it is crossed to an agent for collection being a banker, the banker on whom it is drawn shall refuse payment thereof.
(2) Where the banker on whom a cheque is drawn which is so crossed nevertheless pays the same, or pays a cheque crossed generally otherwise than to a banker, or if crossed specially otherwise than to the banker to whom it is crossed, or his agent for collection being a banker, he is liable to the true owner of the cheque for any loss he may sustain owing to the cheque having been so paid.

Provided that where a cheque is presented for payment which does not at the time of presentment appear to be crossed, or to have had a crossing which has been obliterated, or to have been added or altered otherwise than as authorised by this Act, the banker paying the cheque in good faith and without negligence shall not be responsible or incur any liability, nor shall the payment be questioned by reason of the cheque having been crossed, or of the crossing having been obliterated or having been added to or altered otherwise than as authorised by this Act, and of payment having been made otherwise than to a banker or to the banker to whom the cheque is or was crossed, or to his agent for collection being a banker, as the case may be.

S.80 PROTECTION TO THE BANKER ON PAYMENT OF A CROSSED CHEQUE

Where the banker on whom a crossed cheque is drawn, in good faith, and without negligence pays it, if crossed generally, to a banker, and if crossed specially, to the banker to whom it is crossed, or his agent for collection being a banker, the banker paying the cheque, and, if the cheque has come into the hands of the payee, the drawer, shall respectively be entitled to the same rights and be placed in the same position as if payment of the cheque has been made to the true owner thereof.

The Cheques Act 1957

S.1 PROTECTION TO THE BANKER ON PAYMENT OF AN UNINDORSED OR IRREGULARLY INDORSED CHEQUE

(1) Where a banker in good faith and in the ordinary course of business pays a cheque drawn on him which is not indorsed or is irregularly indorsed, he does not, in doing so, incur any liability by reason only of the absence of, or irregularity in, indorsement, and he is deemed to have paid it in due course.

S.4 PROTECTION TO THE BANKER COLLECTING CHEQUES

(1) Where a banker, in good faith and without negligence:
    (a) receives payment for a customer of an instrument to which this section applies; or
    (b) having credited a customer's account with the amount of such an instrument, receives payment thereof for himself;

and the customer has no title, or a defective title to the instrument, the banker does not incur any liability to the true owner of the instrument by reason only of having received payment thereof.

A banker is not to be treated for the purposes of this section as having been negligent by reason only of his failure to concern himself with the absence of, or irregularity in, indorsement of an instrument.

Companies Act 1985

S.1 COMPANY FORMATION, THE MEMORANDUM OF ASSOCIATION: MODE OF FORMING AN INCORPORATED COMPANY

(1) Any two or more persons associated for a lawful purpose may be subscribing their names to a memorandum of association and otherwise complying with the requirements of this Act in respect of registration, form an incorporated company, with or without limited liability.
(2) A company so formed may be either:
    (a) . . . a company limited by shares
    (b) . . . a company limited by guarantee, or
    (c) . . . an unlimited company.
(3) A 'public company' is a company limited by shares or limited by guarantee and having a share capital, being a company:
    (a) the memorandum of which states that it is to be a public company, and
    (b) in relation to which the provisions of this Act or the form Companies Acts as to the registration or re-registration of a company as a public company have been complied with on or after 22nd December 1980;
    and a 'private company' is a company that is not a public company.
(4) . . . A company cannot be formed as or become a company limited by guarantee with a share capital.

S.2 REQUIREMENTS WITH RESPECT TO MEMORANDUM

(1) The memorandum of every company must state:
    (a) the name of the company;

(b) whether the registered office of the company is to be situated in England and Wales, or in Scotland;

(c) the objects of the company.

. . .

(3) The memorandum of a company limited by shares or by guarantee must also state that the liability of its members is limited

. . .

(5) In the case of a company having a share capital:
  (a) the memorandum must also (unless it is an unlimited company) state the amount of the share capital with which the company proposes to be registered and the division of the share capital into shares of a fixed amount;
  (b) no subscriber of the memorandum may take less than one share.

S.10 DOCUMENTS TO BE SENT TO THE REGISTRAR

(1) The company's memorandum and articles (if any) shall be delivered:
  (a) to the registrar of companies for England and Wales, if the memorandum states that the registered office of the company is to be situated in England and Wales . . . ,
  (b) . . . Scotland, if the memorandum states that the registered office of the company is to be situated in Scotland.

[*Note*: With the memorandum there should be a statement in prescribed form containing the names of the first director(s) and secretary, who should sign on behalf of the subscribers. The company's registered office address should be stated.]

S.518 LIQUIDATING A COMPANY

A company is deemed unable to pay its debts:

(a) if a creditor (by assignment or otherwise) to whom the company is indebted in a sum exceeding £750 then due has served on the company, by leaving it at the company's

registered office, a written demand in the prescribed form requiring the company to pay the sum so due, and the company has three weeks thereafter neglected to pay the sum or to secure or compound for it to the reasonable satisfaction of the creditor, or
(b) if, in England and Wales, execution or other process issued on a judgement decree or order of any court in favour of a creditor of the company is returned unsatisfied in whole or in part, or

. . .

(c) and (d) apply to Scotland and Northern Ireland respectively
(e) if it is proved to the satisfaction of the court that the company is unable to pay its debts.

Consumer Credit Act 1974

CONSUMER CREDIT AGREEMENTS

1 A personal credit agreement is an agreement between an individual (the debtor) by which the creditor provides the debtor with credit of any amount.
2 A consumer credit agreement is a personal credit agreement by which the creditor provides the debtor with credit not exceeding £5,000. [*Note*: This figure was raised to £15,000 in 1983.]
3 A consumer credit agreement is a regulated agreement within the meaning of this Act, if it is not an agreement (an 'exempt agreement') specified in or under Section 16.

Data Processing Act 1984

An organization which stores information concerning individuals in computerized files must register as a data user, and must observe the principles laid down in the Act. The seven principles which apply to data users are as follows:

1 The information to be contained in personal data shall be obtained and personal data shall be processed, fairly and lawfully.

2 Personal data shall be held only for one or more specified and lawful purposes.
3 Personal data held for any purpose or purposes shall not be used or disclosed in any manner incompatible with that purpose or those purposes.
4 Personal data held for any purpose or purposes shall be adequate, relevant and not excessive in relation to that purpose or those purposes.
5 Personal data shall be accurate and, where necessary, kept up to date. [*Note*: 'Accurate' means correct and not misleading as to any matter of fact.]
6 Personal data held for any purpose or purposes shall not be kept for longer than is necessary for that purpose or those purposes.
7 An individual shall be entitled:
  (a) at reasonable intervals and without undue delay or expense –
    (i) to be informed by any Data User whether he holds personal data of which that individual is the Subject, and
    (ii) to access to any such data held by a Data User; and
  (b) where appropriate to have such data corrected or erased.

[This last principle introduces the right of subject access which is fully described in Section 21 of the Act. Requests shall be met in forty days after receipt. Note also the Secretary of State will make an order fixing the maximum fee which may be charged for subject access, thus ensuring that no 'undue expense' is incurred by data subjects. If the data are already covered by the Consumer Credit Act, for example information held by Credit Reference Agencies, the data are exempt from this Act's requirements.]

The Insolvency Act 1985

S.2 QUALIFICATION OF A PRACTITIONER

(1) Any person who acts as an insolvency practitioner in

relation to a company or an individual at a time when he is not qualified to do so shall be liable:
(a) on summary conviction, to imprisonment for a term not exceeding 6 months or to a fine not exceeding the statutory maximum or to both;
(b) on conviction or indictment, to imprisonment for a term not exceeding 2 years or to a fine or to both.

(2) A person acts as an insolvency practitioner in relation to a company by acting
   (a) as its liquidator, administrator or administrative receiver, or
   (b) as supervisor of a composition or scheme approved by it under this Act.

(3) A person acts as an insolvency practitioner in relation to an individual by acting
   (a) as his trustee in bankruptcy or interim receiver of his property or as permanent or interim trustee in the sequestration of his estate;
   (b) as a trustee under a deed which is a deed of arrangement for the benefit of his creditors;
   (c) As supervisor of a composition or scheme proposed by him and approved under this Act.

S.4 DUTY OF COURT TO DISQUALIFY UNFIT DIRECTOR OF INSOLVENT COMPANIES

(1) The court shall make a disqualification order against a person in any case where, on an application under this section, the court is satisfied
   (a) that he is or has been a director of a company which has at any time become insolvent (whether while he was a director or subsequently), and
   (b) that his conduct as a director of that company (either taken alone or taken together with his conduct as a director of any other company or companies) makes him unfit to be concerned in the management of a company.

(2) The period . . . of disqualification . . . shall not be less than 2 years.

5.15 THE OFFENCE OF 'WRONGFUL TRADING'

A director may be liable for a contribution to company assets if . . .
. . .
(2)(b) at some time before the commencement of the winding up of the company, that person knew or ought to have concluded that there was no reasonable prospect that the company would avoid going into solvent liquidation . . . [and that person was a director of the company at that time].

The Supply of Goods and Services Act 1982

S.13 In a contract for the supply of a service, where the supplier is acting in the course of a business, the supplier is obliged to carry out the service with reasonable skill and care.

S.14 where the contract for the supply of a service by a supplier acting in the course of a business, the time of performance is not specified, then the supplier is obliged to carry out the service within a reasonable period of time.

S.15 where the consideration or the manner in which it is to be determined is not dealt with by the contract or is not determined by a course of dealing between the parties, there is an implied term that the purchase will pay a reasonable price.

The Unfair Contract Terms Act 1977

Excluding liability for negligence:

S.2(1) A person cannot by reference to any contract term or to notice given to persons generally or to particular persons exclude or restrict his liability for death or personal injury resulting from negligence.

S.2(2) In the case of other loss or damage, a person cannot so exclude or restrict his liability for negligence except in so far as the term or notice satisfies the requirement of reasonableness.

2.3 Liability between contracting parties where one deals on the others written standard terms of business:

... The party cannot by reference to a contract term ... exclude or restrict any liability in respect of the breach [of contract] ... except in so far as the contract terms satisfies the requirements of reasonableness. [*Note*: Statute also makes an exclusion clause void if it attempts to limit ss.12–15 of the Sale of Goods Act 1979; similar provision is made for the consumer protection clauses in the Supply of Goods and Services Act 1982.]

GUIDELINES FOR APPLICATION OF THE REASONABLENESS TEST

Matters to which regard is to be had ... are any of the following which appear to be relevant:

(a) The strength of the bargaining positions of the parties relative to each other, taking into account (among other things) alternative means by which the customer's requirements could have been met;
(b) whether the customer received an inducement to agree to the term, or in accepting it had an opportunity of entering into a similar contract with other persons, but without having to accept a similar term;
(c) whether the customer knew or ought reasonably to have known of the existence and extent of the term having regard, among other things, to any custom of the trade and any previous course of dealings between the parties;
(d) where the term excludes or restricts any relevant liability if some condition is not complied with, whether it was reasonable at the time of the contract to expect that compliance with that condition would be practicable;
(e) whether the goods were manufactured, processed or adapted to the special order of the customer.

Appendix III: Specimen examination paper

The Institute of Bankers

BANKING CERTIFICATE—PRELIMINARY SECTION

STAGE 1

THE BUSINESS OF BANKING

15 May 1987

N.B. 1. Read the instructions on the cover of the answer book.

2. **Answer ALL questions in Section A—one mark per question.**

   Answer FOUR questions in Section B—20 marks for each question. When questions in Section B are subdivided, each part carries an equal share of the total marks for that question.

3. Time allowed: THREE Hours.

SECTION A

Answer ALL questions in this section

For Questions 1–9, write A, B, C or D in the answerbook.

1.—Which one of the following statements is correct?

A. Cheques are defined as money.
B. Cheques are legal tender.

C. Bank deposits are money but are not legal tender.
D. Bank deposits are not money but are legal tender.

2.—Which one of the following is not a bank financial intermediary?

A. National Westminster Bank
B. National Savings Bank
C. National Girobank
D. TSB (Trustee Savings Bank)

3.—Which one of the following characteristics of a banker has not been identified by English case law?

A. Crediting money and cheques
B. Granting loans
C. Debiting accounts
D. Keeping accounts

4.—Which one of the following is an incorrect endorsement of a cheque under English law?

A. Payee Dr J Brown endorsed James Brown Dr
B. Payee Dr J Brown endorsed Dr James Brown
C. Payee Mrs Alice Jones endorsed A Jones
D. Payee Mrs Alice Jones endorsed Alice Jones

5.—The Consumer Credit Act regulates loans up to what amount?

A. £ 5,000
B. £10,000
C. £15,000
D. £20,000

6.—Which one of the following services is not provided by ATM's?

A. Request for a cheque book
B. Cash withdrawal
C. Setting up a loan or overdraft
D. Statement request

230 The business of banking

7.—What is the maximum period of 'free credit' a customer can obtain when using a credit card in the U.K.?

A. 14 days
B. 28 days
C. 30 days
D. 56 days

8.—Town clearing deals with cheques of more than what amount?

A. £   1,000
B. £ 10,000
C. £ 50,000
D. £100,000

9.—Which one of the following characteristics does not apply to National Savings services?

A. Tax deducted at source
B. Government guarantees
C. Small amounts from individuals
D. Fixed rates of interest

10.—Give two functions of money.

11.—Name two short-term money markets.

12.—Name two banker/customer relationships.

13.—Give two reasons why people save.

14.—Give two reasons why banks take references on customers.

15.—Name two documents the bank would want to see when opening an account for a public limited company.

16.—Complete the following sentence using no more than 12 words:

'*Ultra vires* lending is . . . .'

17.—State two of the types of endorsement.

18.—Write the following sentence in full including the omitted word:

'Account Payee' is an instruction to the .... banker.

19.—State two of the benefits to the borrower of an endowment mortgage.

20.—Give two reasons why the building societies are the banks' greatest competitors.

SECTION B

Answer FOUR questions from this section.

21.—What qualities must money possess? Discuss how these qualities are found in today's money.
[20]

22.—The activities of the banking sector impinge on all our lives. Briefly outline these activities and show how they affect us.
[20]

23.—Banks apply different considerations to different types of customer. Give examples of these special considerations for each main type of customer. Briefly explain the importance of the considerations to a banker.
[20]

24.—The nature of the relationship a banker has with his customer can vary according to the type of transaction involved. Give details of these relationships and the bankers' rights and duties involved.
[20]

25.—(a) What is the practical effect of crossing a cheque?
 (b) Explain the types of crossing that appear on cheques.
 (c) What is the effect of adding the words 'account payee' to a crossed cheque?
[20]

232 The business of banking

26.—You have been invited to the local college to talk to students about bank services that could be useful to them.
What services would you talk about and what customer benefits would you mention? You have just 20 minutes for the talk and can only cover the main services.

[20]

27.—'Moving paper around the banking system is an expensive way of transacting business.'
Explain some of the methods and systems that are available to cut down on this movement of paper.

[20]

28.—What financial service or services would you suggest for the following people? State the benefits to the customer of the services to help explain your choice.

(a) Dave Smith is becoming a little worried about his financial future. He hasn't saved much in the past but he thinks he could at present afford to put aside £30 a month, although he expects to be able to save more next year. Dave has a steady job and his salary is paid into his account monthly. Although he is not too knowledgeable about financial matters he does worry about the effects of inflation. Dave pays tax at the standard rate.

(b) Elaine Wilson is a 28 year old teacher who has two children aged 8 and 6. Unfortunately, her husband died when the children were very young and Elaine is now left to bring up her family on her salary alone. She is concerned about what will happen to the children should anything happen to her. The children would live with her parents but they might have financial difficulties in supporting them. Elaine is very keen on the children's education and would like to give them a sum of money to help them through university.

(c) Jane and Peter Fitzgerald are a newly married couple who are hoping to buy their own house. They are both aged 22 and work for the local council. They will be able to save £150 a month for the next year or two, which they hope will give them a deposit for their house.

(d) Anne Smythe has recently retired and receives a monthly pension cheque from her employer to add to her state pension. Anne lives in a small village some 10 miles from the nearest town and, as she does not own a car, she does most of her shopping in the village store which doubles as a post office. She does, however, go into town once a month to the large supermarket to buy any special items that she cannot get in the village.

Anne lives on her own and has to organise her finances to pay the usual household bills.

[20]

Index

acceptance houses 20
accounts: operating the account –
  bankruptcy of account holder 40,
  42, 55, 68; breaking the account
  39–40, 42; checking procedures
  36–7; closing the account 54, 58;
  death of account holder 37, 40, 55,
  68; dormant accounts 55; mental
  incapacity 37, 40, 42, 55; types of –
  business 40–4, company 42–4,
  partnership 41–2, 48, sole trader
  40–1, 102; budget 49, 92; building
  society 45; current 22, 46–7, 48, 52,
  54, 60, 66, 90, 91; deposit 47–9, 52;
  home mortgage 92–6; individual
  see personal; interest earning 47–9;
  joint 39–40, 48, 101; loan 38, 49–50,
  54, 91; local authority 44; minors
  38–9; personal 36–8, 40, 48, 69;
  revolving credit 92; savings 48;
  voluntary organizations 44–5
account payee 76
administrator 45, 120
advances *see* lending; overdrafts
agency law 60–4
agent for collection 2, 136
Annual Percentage Rate (APR) 50
Articles of Association 43, 44, 101
asset: balance sheet 31; management
  service 111; money as an 24;
  personal 44
Association of Payment Clearing
  Services (APACS) 23, 138
automated teller machines (ATM) *see*
  cash dispenser

bailment 64–5
bailor/bailee *see* bailment
banks 15–23, 52; collecting 37, 66,
  70–1, 72, 74, 139, 146, 148, 149;
  definition of 52; foreign 17–19, 165;
  growth of 15–23; history of 1–14;
  merchant banks 20; paying banks
  66, 70–1, 74, 82, 84, 139; secondary
  banks 21

Bank Charter Act 7, 9, 28
banker/customer relationship 38,
  52–60
Bankers' Books Evidence Act 56
banker's draft 87–8
bank giro 86–7, 149
bank statements 46–7, 48, 120
Banking Act 12, 22, 34, 52, 56,
  168–70
Bank of England 4–13, 31–4, 139,
  163, 175–6; banking department
  7–9; bestowing of banking status
  12, 168–70, 171; control of
  banking system 162–8; directives
  12, 13, 33, 89, 164, 172; functions
  of 5, 10–13; issue department 7–8;
  notes 7, 11, 28, 30, 126; supervision 12–13, 34, 87, 172–4
Bank of England Nationalization Act
  10, 34, 172
bankrupt 3, 36, 45
barter 24–5
base rates 91, 166
bills of exchange 2, 20, 35, 75, 77–81,
  130–1
Bills of Exchange Act 52, 77, 78, 80,
  130, 145, 168
broker *see* stockbroker
building societies 35, 45, 48, 74–5,
  76, 92, 95, 153, 179–84
business accounts *see* accounts,
  types of
business advisory services 116

CAMPARI 105
cash: dispenser 46, 70, 82–3, 158–60;
  management service 115–16, 121
certificates of deposit 35, 176
Certificate of Incorporation 44
cheques 35, 67, 140, 141; altering a
  cheque 58, 68, 146; bearer cheque
  58, 70, 75, 145; collecting a cheque
  52, 54, 61, 63; countermand of a
  cheque 55, 68, 71, 146; crossings
  75–7, 145–6; current uses of 81;

dishonour of 72–3; drawing a 32, 55, 68–9, 86, 143–7; encashment of 69–70; forged signature on 59, 68–9; legal bar to payment 55, 147; mutilated cheques 146; non-payment of 71–2, 148–9; parties to 70; open cheques 75; payment of 61, 63; post dated 68, 145; signature on 68; stopping a 55, 69, 71–2, 74, 76; travellers 23, 35; uncrossed 72; wages 69
cheque book 37, 46, 48, 49, 54, 60, 66, 69, 70, 81–2, 113, 120, 157
cheque card 46, 48, 54, 60, 66, 69, 72, 81–2, 113, 146–7, 156
Cheques Act 37
clearing 11, 12, 70, 75, 136–8; Bankers Automated Clearing Services Ltd (BACS) 83, 138, 153–4; CHAPS and Town Clearing Co. Ltd 138, 150–1; Cheque and Credit Clearing Co. Ltd 138–9, 149–50; Committee of London Clearing Banks 137; Committee of London and Scottish Banks (CLSB) 138, 155; house 137; procedures 139–41
coins 26–7, 31–2
Coinage Act 1971 27
company *see* registered company
Companies Act 43, 57, 89, 191
computer services 116–17
confidentiality *see* secrecy
Consumer Credit Act 50, 89, 90, 92, 101–4, 168, 170
contract law 38, 53–8, 67; breach of 53, 73; contract of agency 60–4; contract of bailment 64–5; contract of guarantee 38, 57, 104
conversion 63, 65, 76, 109
credit 55, 70, 106, 130, 165; in credit 46, 55, 60; credit scoring 99
credit cards 35, 104, 105–7, 155, 194
creditor 54–5, 56, 83, 84, 130
current account *see* accounts, types of
customers of a bank: legal duties of 58–9; types of *see* accounts, types of

debit 47, 55, 70, 140, 143, 148
debtor 54–5, 67, 83, 85, 130
defamation, tort of 56
demand (for borrowing) 32, 33
depositors 28, 31, 170
deposits 20, 31–2, 108, 110; deposit account 47–9, 52; special deposits 33–4
direct debits 83, 85–6, 154
directives *see* Bank of England, directives
disclaimer 56, 59, 111
disclosure 56
documentary credits 132–3
double coincidence of wants 24–5
drawee 70, 80, 130; drawee bank 71, 75, 140
drawer 70, 71, 73, 74, 75, 81, 130
duties of a banker 54–8
duties of a customer 58–9

EFT-POS (Electronic Funds Transfer Point of Sale) 35, 138, 154–7
endorsement 67, 71, 73, 74–5
exchange control 127, 147, 165, 192
Exchange Control Act 147, 168
exchange rates 126, 129, 130, 164
executor 45, 97, 102, 119–20, 123

factoring 118–19
Family Law Inheritance Act 120
financial advice 52
foreign currency 126–7, 129
foreign exchange facilities 23, 52, 129–30
forged signatures 47, 68–9, 144
forgery, prevention of 54, 59–60
free banking 60

garnishee order 55, 69, 147
goldsmiths 3, 4, 28
guarantee card *see* cheque card

hire purchase 115
holder 70, 74, 131
'holder in due course' 77
home banking 120–2

income tax service 120
indemnity clause 38–9
individual accounts *see* accounts, types of
indorsement *see* endorsement
Infants Relief Act 38
insurance 91, 93, 113–14, 188–9
interest 48, 49, 60, 89, 106
interest earning cheque accounts 47

interest rates 13, 33, 46, 85, 121, 162–3, 166, 175–6
investments: advice 59, 110; services 110–11
investment trusts 191–2

joint accounts *see* accounts, types of

leasing 117–18
lending 31–2, 89–107, 108; basics of 89–90; lending to companies 101–2, 178–9; lending directives 89, 164; lending facilities, 90–6; factors that affect lending 98–101; lending for home buying 92–6; reasons for borrowing 96–8
liability, joint and several 39–40, 41–2
liabilities 31, 44
libel 73
licensed deposit takers 21, 52, 162
limited company *see* registered company
limited liability 5, 44
liquidator 45
liquidity 24; ratios 163, 166
loans 22, 23, 31–2, 52, 56, 60, 89–107, 114–15, 178; accounts 49–50; interest 89, 90, 91–3
London Discount Market 34

mandate form 39, 43, 45, 52, 63, 109, 143, 144
markets: eurocurrency 18; foreign exchange 18, 173; money 23
Memorandum of Association 43, 44, 101
Mental Health Act 38
Minimum Lending Rate 166, 171
money 24–35; boxes 48; creating money 32; development of paper money 27–8; functions of 28–30; properties of 30–1; shops 21, 198–9; transmission services 108
Moneylenders Act 168
mortgages 60, 93–6, 182

national debt 6
National Savings Certificates 184–5
negligence, tort of 37, 56, 65, 76, 109, 110
negotiable instruments 73–5, 131
night-safe 108

notes: bank notes 4, 5, 26, 28; note issue 5, 7, 11, 31–2
not negotiable 75, 76

one-stop banking 108
open market operations 13, 34, 171, 173
overdrafts 46, 52, 54, 56, 58, 60, 72, 73, 90–1, 146

PARSAR 105
partnerships 41–2, 48, 61, 114
Partnership Act 42
payee 67, 70, 72, 73, 74, 80, 131, 145
paying in 46, 66
paying-in book 37, 47, 48, 74
personal identification number (PIN) 83, 155, 160
personal representatives 37, 45
power of attorney 61–2
Prevention of Fraud (Investment) Act 1958 170
Protection of Depositors Act 168

receiver 38
references 37
'refer to drawer' 72–3, 148
registered company 42–4, 61, 101–2, 114, 175, 178–9

safe custody 64–5, 109–10
safe deposit 110
safe-keeping 1, 66
secrecy, bankers' duties of 47, 54, 57–8, 63
security 50, 91, 93, 100–1
settlement 152, 154
shareholders 42
shares 61, 63, 190–1
signatures: on cheques 47, 68–9, 81, 143; specimens 37, 69
sole trader 40–1, 74, 102, 108, 114
special crossing 77
special deposits 13, 33–4, 173
standing orders 55, 83–5, 153
status 36–7
status enquiry 56
stockbroker 24, 59, 62, 109, 110–11, 190
Stock Exchange 20, 24, 116
Supply of Goods And Services Act 59–60

Taxes Management Act 57
travellers cheques 127–8
Treasury 33, 173
Treasury bills 35, 163, 166, 175–6
truncation 150
trustees 39, 48, 102
trustee and executor services 119–20
trustee in bankruptcy 40, 45

unlisted securities market 20

Unfair Contract Terms Act 59, 111
unit trusts 22, 112–13, 192–3

voluntary organizations, accounts of *see* accounts, types of

'walks' system 137
wealth 3, 24, 27; personal wealth of partners 41
winding up 55
withdrawing 46